Listen for a change

LISTEN
for a
change

compiled by Annejet Campbell

GROSVENOR

LONDON MELBOURNE WELLINGTON RICHMOND VA

First published 1986
GROSVENOR BOOKS,
54 Lyford Road, London, SW18 3JJ

21 Dorcas Street, South Melbourne
Victoria 3205, Australia

PO Box 1834, Wellington,
New Zealand.

GROSVENOR USA
PO Box 8647,
Richmond, VA 23226.

US Trade Distributor:
M & B Fulfillment Service Inc.,
540 Barnum Avenue,
Bridgeport, Conn. 06608

© Annejet Campbell
Designed by Margaret Gray

British Library Cataloguing in Publication Data

Listen for a change
1. Marriage
I. Campbell, Annejet
306. 8'1'0922   HQ734

ISBN 1-85239-001-8
ISBN 1-85239-000-X Pbk

Library of Congress Catalog
Pre-assigned Card Number 86-81348

Phototypeset by Input Typesetting Ltd., London, SW19
Printed and bound in Malta
by Interprint Ltd., Valletta.

Contents

Acknowledgments

I want to thank Diana Bennett and Pat Ducé as well as other friends for the untiring support and wise counsel they gave me while I was working on this book.

It was Diana who first had the idea that a book of this kind was needed. Both she and Pat spent many hours reading, working and commenting on the stories as they came in.

My special gratitude goes to Mary Lean for her invaluable input and her skilful editing, and to Margaret Gray who took on the delicate job of taking and finding the right photographs to go with each chapter.

Most of all I want to thank all those who took the time and trouble to make their stories available. Without them there would be no book at all.

And last but not least I thank Paul, Edith Anne and Digna for their tremendous support throughout this venture, and for their honesty and sense of humour which kept me down to earth.

Preface

Two years ago Paul and I celebrated our Silver Wedding.

Sometimes I feel amazed that two such different people have been able to enjoy each other's company for so long. Paul is a doctor, born and raised in the Canadian prairies. His only sister died when she was five. I am Dutch, one of seven children, and I studied fashion in Amsterdam and Paris. We now live in London. We hardly knew each other when we got married – and we still approach most issues from different angles.

The most important ingredient in our marriage has been our common commitment. Before we met, we had each made a contract with God – giving Him our lives to use in any way He could to help bring about the changes which are so badly needed in the world.

More and more people are getting married every day – and more and more marriages are breaking up. The divorce rate in the USA has more than doubled in the last 15 years and one in three marriages in Canada and Britain ends in divorce. Paul and I have not had traumatic upheavals in our marriage, but many of our friends have not been so fortunate. Seeing their pain and despair made me want to put together this book.

For, in spite of the depressing statistics, I know many couples who have found reconciliation, some after months of separation or years of divorce. They have found that marriage can be exciting and satisfying and that instead of changing partners, it is possible for both partners to change. There is a price to pay, but it is worth it.

In this book some of these people tell their stories. They include people like Mario and Linda, who were fighting over their children in the street; James and Barbara, who hardly spoke to each other for six years; Daniel and Elaine, who split up when she had an affair; Jacques and Francine, who didn't fight but knew something was dividing them; and Lucy, a battered wife who has rebuilt her life after divorce. The common thread which

Annejet and Paul Campbell

A D Webster

runs through many of their experiences is the discovery that God can show us what to do if we are willing to listen to Him and obey.

Most of these people are personal friends of mine and all the stories are true. For the sake of anonymity, I have changed many of the names. None of the people mentioned in the book appears in the photographs which illustrate it.

Margaret Gray

Chapter 1

Can you hear me?

A few years ago Paul and I had supper with some Canadian friends. 'What would you say your purpose in life was?' I asked the husband. He said he had never thought about it – but it started him talking. Towards the end of the evening his wife said to him, 'Tonight you've talked more deeply than in all our twenty years of marriage.'

Communication is the rock on which many good marriages founder. Paul and I have to work at it every day. When we first married he would sometimes go into a silent mood which could last for days on end, while I went up the wall with frustration. Finally, when I could not stand it any longer, I would ask, 'What on the earth is the matter?'

'Oh, nothing,' he would say.

'But you haven't said anything for three days.'

'Oh, haven't I?' He wasn't even aware of his silence. Then I would begin asking questions and eventually we would discover what had annoyed him three days before and caused the silence. Sometimes it turned out to be something quite insignificant and we would have a good laugh together.

Night shift Some couples begin to drift apart when something happens which seems too painful to talk about. When Joe and Jenny, a British couple, lost their only son, Peter, in Northern Ireland, their marriage nearly died with him. Jenny writes:

You never think it will happen to you, but the fear of it constantly nags inside you. Joe had wanted Peter to go into the army; I was not so keen. So when he was killed, Joe felt I blamed him. He went silent and turned inward, convincing himself that I hated him.

We had had 19 happy years as a family.

1

Joe had been in the army for 15 years before we married, and the first five years of our marriage, I felt, were dominated by it. I was relieved when he left and got a good job, when Peter was 18 months old. I had had two previous miscarriages before he was born, and lost another baby two years later, so Peter was very important to us. It was agonising when he died so young.

I suppose I did blame Joe really. I felt he should have left the boy to make up his own mind instead of filling his head with an unrealistic view of army life. When Peter joined the army he became regimented and a little 'outside' the family. Before that we had enjoyed each other's company and pastimes.

I could see the pain in Joe's eyes and he could probably see it in mine. But rather than face each other's suffering, we drifted farther and farther apart. In the end we were on the brink of divorce. Joe had a girl-friend and I had my nursing. He was out during the day and I was working four nights a week.

One night I was working in intensive care. One of the men on the critical list was Joe's age, with his build and hair colour. When I looked at his records I saw that he had been through a traumatic divorce recently and that his present condition was due to attempted suicide. In fact, he died later that week.

I was really shaken. What if that happened to Joe? What if his silent brooding had developed into severe depression and he was considering ending it all because of Peter's death and my attitude towards him?

I spent that night in turmoil, my imagination running riot. In the end I rang him to see if he was all right. He was amazed. I blurted out something over the phone and he said something back – I can't remember what. Before I realised it we were both in tears. Sister came in and told me to pull myself together as she didn't want any patients drowned!

Next day Joe stayed home from work and we talked and talked; how Peter's death had hurt us; what we felt now. Feelings fell over themselves to be expressed. I don't know exactly what happened, but once we started talking to each other and found the courage to speak of all the pent-up hurts, a great healing began to take place. Life is very different now.

Everything going my way

When Canadians Pierre and Sara married, he was studying for a doctorate in industrial relations. 'A job was waiting for me after my studies,' he says. 'Everything seemed to be going my way.' Sara's work as a lawyer was less satisfying and she was becoming discontented.

'I found out later that Sara felt like a ship adrift,' Pierre goes on. 'I thought she was suffering from apathy. She thought my interest in my work meant I was indifferent to her. Poor communication between us was breeding a separation. We ended up living apart for several months.'

When Sara left, Pierre was shell-shocked and became depressed. 'I just couldn't understand what had hit me. I normally throw myself into activity to avoid facing reality, but this time, with the help of a marriage guidance counsellor and of friends, I started to take a fresh look at myself.

'I began to realise that I had been blaming Sara for everything that had gone wrong. She had told me I was not to blame and I felt very self-righteous. Now I saw that I had not listened to her or recognised her silent plea for help. It was painful to accept my share of the responsibility, but once I did, my whole attitude changed.'

For over a year they had a weekend relationship, living in different cities, with Pierre dividing his time between the two. Slowly they put the pieces of their marriage together again – and built something different from what they had had before.

They now live in an old farmhouse in Quebec which they have restored themselves and after ten years of marriage have had a baby daughter. 'My work no longer has a higher priority than my family,' says Pierre. They do voluntary work together – running a pack of Cubs and organising an appeal for clothes for people in the West Indies. 'We try to be in tune with other people's needs and to respond to them,' says Pierre.

Baby barrier

Jacques and Francine couldn't understand what was coming between them. Then, on holiday in the mountains far from their busy life in Paris, they had time to talk. Francine remembers:

It was a beautiful moonlit night and the atmosphere was relaxed. Jacques and I began to talk together as we had not for a very long time. Since our first child, Eliane, was born eight years before, there had been a barrier between us. I had puzzled about it many times.

That night I began to understand what had happened. I had loved and admired Jacques since I was 18. Our meeting had been providential and had changed our lives completely. The arrival of our baby, although it gave me a reason for living, seemed to complicate things. Jacques only had eyes for her, she was his little angel. I was no longer the only one he loved. I felt frustrated, as if something had been taken away from me.

Four years later Suzanne was born. I only

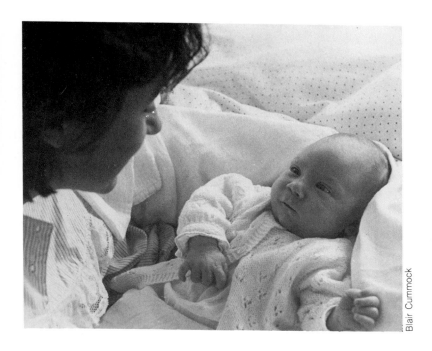

Blair Cummock

'The arrival of our baby, although it gave me a reason for living, seemed to complicate things.'

had love for her. I believed Jacques did not love Suzanne as much as Eliane. So Suzanne became my protégée, which hurt Eliane. She was always wrong in my eyes – and this probably made Jacques love her all the more.

As we talked, we got this situation sorted out. I spoke to Eliane the next morning. I told her everything and asked her to forgive me. Her reaction was instant and radiant, 'At last you've admitted it. You did love Suzanne more than me. I knew it!' And she gave me a big hug. When our third daughter was born we were all able to welcome her and love her without reservation.

Taken for granted

Doug is a British trade union official. 'I fell in love with Sally the first time I saw her,' he says. 'I still remember her coming down the stairs in her mother's house, her blue eyes sparkling with life. I decided there and then that she was the girl I was going to marry!'

That was some 30 years ago. Recently Doug found himself in India on New Year's Eve, as part of a trade union delegation. Although he was at a conference centre full of people, he felt dreadfully alone. He found himself thinking about his marriage in a way he hadn't for a long time.

'I realised I had taken Sally for granted in recent years, though I was still in love with her,' he says. 'When we were first married I often took her out. We were both young and working and we enjoyed ourselves. We discussed everything together. Then the children came along and we weren't able to do so much together. I got busier with my work and left Sally to cope. Gradually I stopped telling her what was on my mind and I expected her to sort out the problems which arose with the children.

'Here I was in India, a militant trade unionist who could call men out on strike whenever I wanted, yet I was utterly lost without my wife. I decided that I owed her an apology. I wrote and told her all that she meant to me and how sorry I was for taking her for granted all these years. Things were quite different when I got back; we talked over everything and I am determined not to slip back into my old complacency.'

Double-talk

Thinking you know what your partner feels isn't the same as really listening to him or her. This is particularly important when one partner is quick and articulate and the other is quieter and more thoughtful.

My friend Diana tells a story against herself about the evening her husband came home exhausted and started doing some gardening. She insisted he came in for supper, thinking she was being helpful, because he clearly needed a nice sit-down. He, on the other hand, was furious – he'd been sitting down all day and found gardening much more relaxing!

'He used to find it infuriating, too, when I gave him a list of suggestions of what we could do at a weekend,' she goes on. 'Somehow it didn't occur to me that he might have ideas of his own! In fact they're often much better than mine; he thinks more deeply and doesn't act on impulse.'

Pat writes short stories for women's magazines; her husband Dick is a technical author, with a talent for precision. This leaves scope for misunderstandings. 'Dick has a rather logical, ordered mind and disconcertingly tends to take words at their face value,' she explains. 'I, on the other hand, often answer what I feel is the *real* query behind his questions. This is inclined to rattle him.

'Example: He might call out, "Where are you?" I think he probably wants to know what I'm doing, so I reply, "I'm dusting." Or he asks, "What are you doing?" and I reply, "I'm in the dining-room." If he is asked, "Where did you buy these chops?", he says, "At so-and-so's in the High Street." The same question addressed to me is more likely to bring the reaction: "Why? What's wrong with them?"

'There are many decisions to make jointly. But there's a time and place for everything – I'd rather not discuss holiday plans in the middle of the trauma of dishing up a major meal; he'd rather not embark on them just as *Match of the Day* is beginning. We have also

7

found that it is worth sticking at a thing until a definite decision is reached; rather than leaving the matter in the air with occasional nibbles at it at odd moments.'

Background music

Some women complain that their husbands are too quiet; some men that their wives are too talkative. The Swiss psychiatrist Paul Tournier was asked about this after a talk he gave in 1982. He replied:

You know how it goes – the man comes home from work looking worried. His wife jumps straight in: 'What's the matter with you? Is something bothering you?' He grunts, 'No.'

A bit later she says, 'Listen, I only need to look at you to see that something's on your mind. We're together for better, for worse. I want to help. I love you. What's the matter?'

'Nothing.'

They sit down to eat. The children are told to keep quiet because Daddy has had a hard day at the office. . .

Then the kids are sent to bed and they are alone together. She starts again. He says, 'I told you! You're annoying me with your questions. You're imagining things.' The more she insists, the more he resists.

As a doctor, I see many wives who tell me, 'I don't seem to be able to have a real conversation with my husband.' When I see the husband later, I say, 'Your wife says she can't talk with you. Why not?' The husband says, 'That's silly. We talk about everything.'

And it's true – they do talk about everything, objectively. They talk about Afghanistan, the price of potatoes, world finance, the children's careers. They talk about everything – but about nothing personal.

This happens to countless couples. The more the wife wants a proper dialogue, the

8

more she wants her husband to say something about his hopes and worries, the more he closes up.

There are many homes where the wife talks all the time. Women tell me, 'I can talk all evening without my husband saying one word. He sits behind the paper and from time to time I say, "Are you listening?", and he says, "Mmm", so I go on.'

I was always lecturing my wife. She had less education than I, so I explained things to her – scientific and psychological subjects, for instance. The thought that *she* might actually have something to teach *me* took me by surprise!

It was really only when we began to listen to the 'inner voice' together that I began to appreciate the importance of what she said, and gave her a chance to express herself. She taught me to respect the whole person. Respect means feeling really equal – expecting to receive as much from the other person as you can give them yourself.

How many men let their wives run on like background music? People joke about women who talk all the time, but they go on doing it because men don't really listen.

Hearing aid   I find that Paul begins to open up about his deeper feelings when I begin to tell him about mine. Communication, for us, starts early in the morning. I love to sleep late, but at around 6.30 or 7.00 a.m. Paul brings me a cup of black coffee to wake me up. Then we give God time to show us what He wants us to do – listening quietly for the 'inner voice', as Paul Tournier calls it.

We write down the thoughts that come to us – mundane or inspired. Sometimes it's simple housekeeping details, sometimes the things that have been worrying me, ideas about how I could have done better yesterday, thoughts on how to help a friend in difficulties. Then we tell each other what we have written.

This morning time of quiet helps us to talk about the things that really matter – and obeying the ideas that come provides adventure in our lives. We find that life never gets stale that way. Many of the people who tell their stories in this book have found the same thing.

Chapter 2

Dream marriages

Most people embark on marriage with high expectations – if not a few illusions. Some relationships don't survive the first shock of reality. 'Ours was a love marriage,' says a politician's wife. 'It started way up high and it was beautiful. In three or four years we had come down to rock bottom.'

When illusion hits reality, there's a temptation to replace the old dream with a new one. I used to drive home after dropping the girls at school listening to tunes from the 1950s and daydreaming about the men I knew before I met Paul. Soon I would be wondering what would have happened if I had married one of them instead – and comparing Paul with them. It seemed innocent enough – except that it divided me from Paul.

My friend Amy had the same experience. After a few years of marriage, she began to find life monotonous. 'I had the husband and children I had always wanted, but now the flavour had gone and my married life had become insipid. I began to wonder what it would be like to be swept off my feet by some Prince Charming and to travel the world happily ever after.'

One day it bore in on her that she had accepted marriage 'till death do us part'. 'I could choose to waste my years on daydreams never to become a reality or I could decide to love my husband again and have a happy marriage here and now,' she says. 'I asked God to give me new love for Tim. I started to cherish him in a new way and I found that love given is multiplied back.'

Rio romance

Teresa met Carlos in Rio de Janeiro and married him when she was 18, full of illusions about what a marvellous life they would have together. She had been born in Germany and he in Portugal. She soon found out that he had a fixed idea of the sort of wife he wanted her to be. The more he tried to make her conform to his image of her, the more she

Berkertex Brides

resisted. He accused her of being domi-
neering and they started fighting.

She was working as a secretary, while
Carlos worked in hotel management. One day
she went to her boss for a loan and he asked
her why she wanted it. She told him that
Carlos and she had separated and that she
needed the money to rent a flat for the two
children and herself.

'We just don't get on together,' she
explained, bursting into tears. 'He's impossible to live with.' And she told him the whole
story.

Finally her boss said, 'If you want your
husband to change, you may have to start the
process yourself. Have you ever thought that
perhaps you could be wrong somewhere?' He
suggested that when she went home that
evening she might think about it using a four-
point summary of the Sermon on the Mount
as her measuring-rod.

After the children were tucked into bed,
she made herself some strong Brazilian
coffee. Then she did as he had suggested.
She wrote down four headings – 'absolute
honesty', 'absolute purity', 'absolute unsel-
fishness' and 'absolute love' – and she started
to think whether her life matched up to these
ideals.

Slowly a picture of herself emerged which
was very different from the one she had cher-
ished. She was not the loving, patient mother
and wife who was always right in every situation. She was guilty of most of the things of
which she had been accusing Carlos – she was
impulsive, untrustworthy, dishonest about
the money she spent on clothes and make-
up, bad-tempered and too proud to say
sorry. No wonder they couldn't live
together.

'Good heavens!' said her boss when she arrived at work next morning. 'You look years younger!'

Going home on the bus that evening she began to formulate a letter to Carlos telling him where she felt she had failed and asking him to forgive her. She wrote it that night.

As soon as Carlos received the letter he phoned and asked if they could meet. He came over right away with a big bunch of roses, told her how touched he was by her frankness and he, too, apologised. He looked so different that she felt hopeful. They talked for a long time and their unresolved feelings of blame and bitterness began to heal. They decided to start living together again.

'This kind of honesty became the new foundation for our marriage,' she told me later. 'Instead of the emptiness inside which I used to try to fill with a drink or two, I began to feel a growing hope that what we had found could be useful to other couples. This proved true when my sister-in-law got reconciled with her husband after staying with us for two months.

'When I left Carlos I thought I would never be able to love him again. But I have experienced that a power from within can give me a new love for him every day, if I ask for it.'

Nightmare

Peter and Anna seemed to have everything going for them when they married. They were deeply in love and, having met through their church, they felt they had a joint mission in life. But the start of their married life was a 'nightmare'. Anna explains:

We did not reckon on the difficulty of actually living together. The first year was awful.

I was a very independent person and would rush to do things, such as changing a plug, which Peter felt were his job. He would react

15

by criticising me. 'Why haven't you hoovered the stairs properly?' he would ask. This made me furious. We would have terrible rows. Sometimes you could cut the atmosphere with a knife.

Peter often made decisions I disagreed with and he was also untidy. My only way of coping was to lose my temper. Sometimes after a row we wouldn't speak to each other for two days.

The arrival of two daughters did nothing to improve our marriage. There seemed no way to end the cycle of quarrels and silences. Sometimes we would try to patch things up, but then we would bring up the same accusations again. Several times Peter had his bags packed, but he never actually left.

One evening I felt desperate. Leaving the two children in the house I rushed out to see a friend, and poured out all my troubles. After listening to me she said, 'Yes, Peter is far too critical of you; he is awfully untidy. But you have got to do something about your terrible temper.'

I was shattered. My parents had often had rows; neither of them had ever apologised to the other and the rows were often followed by silences. But I realised that I must apologise to Peter. I did, and things improved.

Later we both went to see my friend and her husband and we made a joint decision – for three months Peter would not criticise me and would pick up his clothes, and I would not react to him but would accept him as he was. What started as a trial period became a habit. We found a harmonious way of living together where we could discuss things naturally, no longer trying to score off each other. I even picked up the odd sock he forgot, without noticing I was doing it! We began to show each other appreciation.

16

The other day someone said to me, 'You two really love one another!' I laughed to myself as I thought, 'You wouldn't have said that three years ago.'

After the whirlwind

No one could say Tom and Karen's marriage has been easy. They are both writers, outspoken people who were used to their independence when they met. But after over 20 stormy years they are still together. Karen explains why:

We met in the middle of January, got engaged in May and married in August. It was a passionate romance, but it was a shock when we began our married life together. On the third day of our honeymoon we had a flaming row and Tom shouted, 'Let's get a divorce. What's the use of being married?'

Yet, in spite of ourselves, we are still married! Once after a tremendous crisis Tom took the gold ring off his finger. He had often threatened to throw it away, and sometimes even done so. Now he said, 'This ring has been blessed in front of the altar. Have you thought about that?'

I had thought about it. I went into marriage with the conviction that marriage is a sacrament. I firmly believed that God meant us for each other, but after the first three horrible months I was convinced that sex had been the only reason for my wanting to get married. To my great surprise, when I confessed my misgivings, Tom said, 'If there is anything I am sure of, it is that God meant us for each other.'

Tom is not what you would call a 'believer'; I am the churchgoer in the family. But deep inside him there is a respect for what is sacred. So the sacrament has meant, as far as I can understand it, that an unseen wall around us has sheltered our weak union.

Once my daughter said to me, 'Mum, I get so sad when Dad is harsh to you, because I love you. But it hurts me too when you are unloving towards him, because I also love him.' I asked her to pinch me whenever I behaved in an unloving way towards Tom. I was soon black and blue! Several times a day, sometimes during one meal, she had to pinch me.

I was surprised. I wasn't the mild, sweet loving, patient wife I had imagined I was. I had to start work on my own faults instead of criticising Tom for his.

'After work, there he was, sitting in the kitchen reading the paper with his feet on a chair.'

We have a memo-pad on the kitchen wall where we write down the things we need and anyone who is going near a shop is meant to look at the pad and buy them. Tom never looks at it – he goes and buys all the things

Margaret Gray

18

we don't need! If I get up early and bake bread, feeling very proud of myself, he is sure to go and buy bread at the shop. Or if I make marmalade, next day I see two jars of shop marmalade on the table.

I've had to learn to take this in a positive way! To say, 'Oh how nice of you to think of that,' demands a real change of heart in me, thinking of him first rather than of myself.

The other day our eldest son was due to come home. He doesn't come very often, so I really wanted to make the house beautiful. Before going to work I wanted to start cleaning, but Tom was irritated and nervous. 'Get out!' he shouted. So I went, thinking I'd do it later.

After work, there he was, sitting in the kitchen reading the paper with his feet on a chair. I hate having him in the kitchen when I'm cooking the dinner – and even more so if I'm cleaning the floor at the same time. I got so irritated that my arms started aching. Suddenly he asked, 'Why are you so angry? I can feel all around me how much you hate me.' I swallowed, about to deny it. Then I decided to be honest. 'I find it hard to work when you are sitting there reading the paper,' I said. He didn't move.

By this time I was in such a mood that I had to leave the kitchen. I went out into the hall with the broom. What should I do? Our son would feel the atmosphere immediately.

Prayer seemed to be the only hope. I started slowly moving the broom, praying as I did so. The floor became clean, my heart became free and when I had finished the prayer, my arms didn't ache any more. I went back into the kitchen. Tom had gone. When he came in again we could smile at each other.

A few weeks before that we had had a

serious row. Then it was *Tom* who hated *me*. He was furious because he felt I had gone to Mass one time too many. He said some terrible things. For hours I managed to say nothing, but then I started to resist. He was so furious, he hit me.

This had happened many times before, but this time I thought seriously of leaving him. I felt I couldn't go on being humiliated and I knew the children would understand. But as he was in the house I couldn't make any preparations.

Next morning early I started to walk through the woods near our home. I felt torn to pieces with hate, bitterness and humiliation. My arms were aching.

Suddenly I had the idea of praying the Rosary. I started almost unwillingly. But the more I thought of the life of Jesus and His anguish and humiliation on the Cross, although He was without sin, the more I gathered perspective. During those two hours my whole outlook changed.

I had breakfast with friends and walked home. I was astonished – my feet were so light. My body felt renewed. I couldn't even remember the quarrel. When Tom came home in the evening and shyly said, 'You don't have to eat with me if you don't want to,' I smiled and he looked hopeful. Later that night he apologised deeply. I thanked God in my heart for the way He had renewed me through that prayer.

On another occasion we were building a new guest house, which would also be my working place. Tom doesn't like having my friends in our home. As I was going to provide most of the money for this new house, I said to him, 'Now that we're going to have a guest house I want to invite my friends too.'

'Never,' he answered.

'Well, if you're going to prevent my friends coming to our house, I am not going to provide the money. You can do it yourself,' I said, furious.

He went white. It was going to be a lovely guest house and he had planned it with great joy – and money and houses are important to him. He reached for the phone and said, 'OK. I'll call a lawyer. Then we can discuss our divorce.'

His talk of divorce had never come to anything in the past. But this time I knew he was serious. I had hurt one of the deepest things in his life.

I went to my room and wept. What had happened was wrong. But so was his hatred of my friends. What should I do? I had been reading about Francis of Assisi, a man of peace. I went down on my knees and prayed, 'Please help us. Please save our marriage. Please show me the way.'

My tears stopped. Peace came into my heart. Suddenly a thought flashed into my head, as if someone was saying, 'Go and apologise for your hard words.'

'Oh, no,' I protested. 'Not that.'

I think it was the hardest step I had ever taken, but I did it. 'Will you forgive me for getting so mad?' I asked, feeling stupid. Tom looked amazed, stretched out his hand and said, 'Your friends can come – just let me know beforehand.'

This kind of reconciliation seems like a miracle to me. I can't do it. Tom can't do it. But there is a power which can come and give us both the grace to forgive and forget, if we call upon it. And you can do a lot to keep the grace flowing – small things. For instance, we have our own bedrooms and make our own beds – and sometimes his is unmade all day.

Ocasionally a whisper tells me to make it up with clean sheets. I have to overcome something inside me to do it for him – but it is an act of love.

Tom is a very generous man; although he forgets my birthday and our wedding anniversary, he often comes home with roses or chocolates. He is also a very interesting man – and we have so many interests in common. He respects my work – although he never reads what I write. He can be a wonderful host. For me both the difficult things and the good things have been a gift – one for my development, the other for my joy. We always have a lot to talk about.

I certainly don't love him blindly and wildly like I did when we first met. But love has to develop into a sense of faithfulness and willingness and joy in being together, and this kind of love I certainly have.

Unshared illusions

Hans and Ilse's home in West Germany is the nucleus of an experiment in Christian community living. Hundreds of young people from all backgrounds have stayed with them for different periods, learning how to apply their faith in everyday life and in tackling the problems of society.

They started out on marriage in a fourth floor flat with no bath. Hans's income was small, but they were busy and happy. In spite of this, Ilse found that married life wasn't coming up to her expectations. Hans's concept of marriage clashed with hers. Ilse remembers:

Hans was always thunderstruck when I exploded. I used to blame him for my discontent – 'You never have any time for us. Everything comes before your family. You always leave me to solve our problems.'

He would keep quiet. 'Why don't you say

Laurie Sparham (IFL)

'I felt totally isolated with our children in the middle of a big city.'

something?' I'd demand. 'You've said it all already,' he'd say.

I felt totally isolated with our four children in the middle of a big city, and swamped by the housework. Had I spent all those years studying, to slave over a stove? My mother's life had been quite different. She had had nannies and servants to look after the children and the house so that she could devote her time to my father and their guests. I had pictured my married life like hers – yet here I was, looking after everyone else, with nobody looking after me.

Hans thought all this was quite normal. His job was demanding and he enjoyed it. He was often away at weekends at conferences and seminars. He seemed to feel that the husband's only responsibility was to find the money to look after his family's material needs; coming home now and then to enjoy his nice flat, his patient wife and the development of his children. Meanwhile what I wanted was a man who was there for me, with whom I had real friendship and intellectual companionship.

Before I had fully realised that I was becoming disappointed and bitter, Norwegian friends came to stay with us. The wife helped me a lot with the housework, so we had time to talk. One day she asked me, 'Have you ever thought why you don't like cooking?'

'I don't need to think about that,' I said. 'I can tell you right away. I prefer to do other things.' But she said she meant something different – that if I took time to really think about it quietly, then God might help me to learn something about my character. I had never thought of God in such a personal way before. I decided to give it a try. 'What keeps me from enjoying cooking?' I asked myself.

Suddenly it became clear to me, just as if dark glasses had been taken off my eyes. I realised that the cooking and housework hung like heavy weights round my neck because I felt I was destined for something better in life.

What was the point of housework, I wondered. 'Housework is a means of serving the people who've been entrusted to you,' came an answer. 'This is the way to pass on God's love, by caring for the people who come into your home. He will help you to become humble.' I liked this last thought least of all.

I began to see that whenever women decide consciously and joyfully to care for those who have been entrusted to them, without using them for their own purposes, a power-house of love is created. One housewife and mother put it like this – 'I work in the most important workshop of the atomic age, where the future is being shaped.'

This gave me a new view of my home. I saw that the values I passed on by the way I lived would become the foundation of my children's lives, for good or bad. I could gladly commit my strength to shaping the future in this way – it gave the everyday routine new meaning.

This answered some of my troubles – but I still felt abandoned by Hans.

Then we both went to a conference abroad, leaving the children well cared for in Germany. At the conference my feelings of loneliness grew. The meetings were held in English or French and I felt insecure with my schoolgirl English. Hans had no such inhibitions and had befriended a group of young Africans, so I was often alone.

One morning I met a woman who knew her way about the conference centre. 'I'm looking for my husband once again,' I said to her. 'Tell me,' she asked in a friendly way, 'what are you looking for in your husband?' Off she went, leaving me alone.

I knew the answer right away – 'I look for safety, appreciation and security in him. Without him I feel lost, lonely and insecure.' At the same moment I remembered that I was always telling the girls in the youth group I helped with that security could never be found in a man, only in God.

With these thoughts going round and round in my head I became furious with the woman I had talked to and the whole stupid conference. I wanted to leave, but it didn't work out. Then I got an upset gall-bladder and had to go to bed.

In the quiet of my sickroom it became clear to me that I had put my husband in the place which belongs to God. I had fed on his love and appreciation. It was only in his presence that I had a sense of my own value. He was my idol, but a self-made one. He had to be the way I wanted him to be.

Things were becoming clear to Hans too. He told me, 'I took you into my life when we married in the same way as I took the books you brought with you into my bookcase. I wanted to enrich and complete my life through you. I never for a moment thought that I was also entering your life.'

For the first time we were able to talk honestly about the things which had stood between us and divided our lives into two separate streams. We had much to forgive each other and much to be forgiven for.

The illusions which I had brought into marriage had to be destroyed one by one so that we could find a new, solid foundation. We learnt to trust each other and leave the past behind – and to complement each other. This means making no demands about what my partner should be, but trying to fill any gap in our family circle which he doesn't – or can't – fill.

Chapter 3

Repairs after affairs

Can a marriage survive if one of the partners has been unfaithful? Sometimes the hurts are so deep that the situation seems hopeless. And yet if there is the will to survive and make a new start, the wounds can be healed and the marriage may emerge stronger than it was before. I know many couples who have pulled through this painful experience and are now helping others to do so.

Thrown out

When Daniel discovered that Elaine was seeing another man, he told her to leave the house at once. Daniel was a successful businessman, some ten years older than Elaine, and had given her everything she wanted. They had two young children, a lovely home, and an efficient housekeeper who doted on the children and left them both plenty of time to spend on the golf course. But Elaine was bored – and Daniel became suspicious. He hired a private detective who caught her kissing in the other man's car.

Elaine told me the whole story over a cup of coffee a few days after she had moved out. She felt Daniel treated her like a teenager and that she was not needed at home. She didn't really care for the other man, but he had made life more interesting. Now she had decided not to see him again, but Daniel didn't want her back. 'What can I do?' she asked.

I didn't know what she should do, but I suggested we might be quiet and see if any ideas came to us. We sat in the bustling coffee shop and she wrote down, 'I love my husband. I love my children. We need some-

Margaret Gray

29

thing to live for. How can I make a new start?' She decided to write to Daniel, asking for his forgiveness, and posted the letter the same day.

A few days later she phoned me. There had been no reply. She sounded so desperate and depressed that I was afraid she might try to kill herself. All I could tell her was that I was convinced they would be reunited, that many of their friends were praying for them, and not to give up.

In fact when Daniel had received the letter, he had taken it to his lawyer. 'No woman can change that fast; it's a trick,' said the lawyer. 'Pay no attention.' Daniel told my husband Paul that his pride had been so hurt by Elaine's affair that he just could not forgive her and ask her back, although in his heart he really wanted to.

Christmas came and Elaine spent the day with us, trying not to show how much she missed Daniel and the children. There was no message from them, no flowers, no sign of any affection.

Meanwhile, Paul and Daniel had been meeting. Finally Daniel began to look into his own conscience and it slowly dawned on him that he was partly to blame for what had happened. His paternalistic attitude towards Elaine had shielded her from taking responsibility. He provided amply for his family – but was over-engrossed in making the money to do so. And he often flew to the Bahamas for the weekend to play golf and enjoy the nightclubs, leaving Elaine at home in Canada.

One day Daniel phoned us. 'I hear that Elaine is coming to dinner with you tonight,' he said. 'Don't tell her, but I am coming to fetch her home.'

Elaine came and the minutes crept by. Finally Daniel arrived with a large bunch of flowers. He put his arms round her and they talked. 'I've been so proud, but can we try again?' he asked.

'It's a miracle,' said Elaine, when she phoned us some days later.

Elaine now works in Daniel's office, and they have bought a caravan so that they can have family holidays together. The children are growing up in a secure and happy home.

Floating mine

Roger is an architect, an outgoing, flamboyant character. He and Susan, who is a doctor, had been married for three years when he began to get involved with another woman. At first he was trying to help her cope with the insecurity caused by her own husband's erratic behaviour, but soon the relationship developed into an affair, although, Roger says, he still loved Susan.

'Gradually,' he says, 'a sense of wrong began to overtake me. The affair was exciting, but it was selfish and it would hurt Susan deeply. It jeopardised everything I most wanted – a stable marriage, children and a happy home. After about five months I began to see myself clearly and recognised the need to grow up. I ended the affair, but I said nothing to Susan.'

Although the relationship was over, as time went by Roger felt increasingly uncomfortable about having deceived Susan. 'The secret was a floating mine which would one day blow our marriage apart,' he says. 'I realised that only my genuine and open repentance and Susan's forgiveness would defuse it completely.'

Finding the courage was difficult, but eventually he told her everything. 'She was deeply hurt but she forgave me. Our honesty, trust and love have grown from that moment. This is the rock our marriage is built on. It

'I had to get rid of
my hate.
But how?'

Margaret Gray

32

could easily have been the rock to sink us.'

Since then they have had two children. Together they help to prepare engaged couples who are going to be married in their church.

The other woman

'Words cannot describe how broken, furious and defeated I felt when I discovered, after many years of marriage, that my husband was deceiving me,' says Mary. 'Bit by bit I got the painful truth out of him. At that moment I hated both him and the woman involved.'

Mary's husband was as unhappy as she was and decided to end the affair then and there. 'Strangely enough, this decision restored our love for one another,' Mary says. But forgiving the other woman was another matter.

As a Christian, Mary remembered Jesus's words, 'Love your enemies'. 'I saw that I had to get rid of my hate. But how?' In the end Mary decided to invite the woman to her home. 'I prayed with all my heart that I would be shown what to say. My husband was also praying in another room.

'Then it happened. As we sat there, my hate drained out of me. All I saw was a divorced woman, sad and lonely, and I had only one desire – to tell her about God who can change us and show us His plan for our lives.'

Backpacks

One of my friends entered marriage with an emotional backpack – his hatred for his alcoholic mother, because of the way she had treated his father. He hadn't seen her for five years and he began to take out his unresolved feelings on his wife, becoming violent towards her.

When his wife discovered that he had taken up with another woman, she was ready to throw him out. She came and poured out her heart to me. They had two children, aged seven and five. For their sakes she decided to give him another chance – and see if there was any way, however small, in which she was to blame for what was happening.

The next time we met she told me that she had a very close relationship with one of her sisters. They used to talk everything over together and her husband had felt excluded. Some months before, after they had had a row, she had prayed in desperation, 'O God, why don't You find him another woman?' She wept as she realised how wrong she too had been.

Some time later her husband took her out for dinner on her birthday and at the end of the meal she apologised to him for the ways she felt she had failed him. It was the beginning of something new in their relationship – although they are not out of the wood yet.

Hollywood lovers **Mending a marriage may take many years – as it did for James and Barbara, who live in Hollywood. They met when James, a composer, was working on a film, which had 30 gorgeous blondes in it. Barbara was one of them. James's affair with Liz could have been the final crisis in a marriage which seemed doomed from the start – yet they have just celebrated their 42nd wedding anniversary. They tell their own story:**

Barbara We were married three-and-a-half weeks after our first date. During our courtship we would go out to dinner and James would talk about himself until five in the morning. Then he would go to the studio and start work. He never asked me any questions. When we got married I didn't really know him. He was all surface. He talked to me from Mount Olympus – he was brilliant and I stood in awe of him.

34

I had always been a phoney. I used to carry heavy books under my arm because I wanted people to think I was bright. But he didn't know this – he thought I was pretty super. If he had asked me more questions, he might have found out.

When we got married I discovered he was a workaholic; work was his life. He worked Saturdays, Sundays, nights when we weren't entertaining. We had very little time together.

I got pregnant right away, but I also got very ill. Soon after that we got word that his only and adored brother Dickie had been killed in the war. His mother came to us from New York. I hadn't met her before. Dickie had been her life. She stayed in a motel across the road from us until our daughter was born. She was a dear woman, but I shut her out. I had morning sickness, I didn't understand death and I didn't know how to comfort her. I had my own life to lead.

The same thing happened when our second child was born. James's mother came again and again I shut her out. Shortly after she went home she threw herself out of a window. James was devastated by both deaths, yet because I was thinking only of myself, I didn't give him any support. I don't understand why he stuck with me.

James   I stuck with her because I loved her.

Then she decided our house was too small and she found an enormous mansion in the most fashionable part of Beverley Hills. We put a fortune into redoing it. Later it turned out to be the best financial investment we'd ever made. But while she was doing all the alterations I began to feel I couldn't stand it any longer. I told her it was a huge mistake. As I watched her spend enormous amounts of money I wanted to kill her. I moved across the street to stay in comfort with friends and left her amid the clutter and noise.

35

Barbara   Communication went right out of the door.
Nothing I did was right. There I was with
the children and a governess in the back wing
of the house fighting with workmen, and he
would come over and find fault with
everything.

Soon the house was ready and we were
living in it. But I was hardly ever at home. I
figured the governess would take care of the
kids. And I was very resentful of the time
James was spending everywhere else, except
with me.

James made me go to a psychiatrist – which
I didn't want to do. The psychiatrist kept
saying, 'Do your own thing. You have your
own life to lead.' So I went on ski-ing trips
and there were other men in my life. I was
so filled with guilt and so afraid of being
found out that I began yelling at James and
the kids. This went on for 18 years. I was
smoking three packets of cigarettes a day and
drinking heavily.

Then one day I met some people who told
me, 'If you point your finger at your neighbour, there are three more pointing back at
you.' I began to think what this meant about
my relationship with my family and about the
way I was living. I reckoned that if I could
be that addicted to smoking and drinking, I
could be addicted to anything. So in one fell
swoop I stopped both – and eating too,
because I figured I would get awfully fat
compensating for the cigarettes and alcohol.

My new friends suggested I should put
right everything that I could. When I asked
my children's forgiveness, they refused.
'You'll never change,' they said. 'You'll go
on being the same old screaming witch.' It
was hard because I needed their help.

When I asked James for his forgiveness I
told him a few of the things that I had been

36

doing – as much as I felt I could handle. I thought that would be the end of it – that the rainbow would come out and we'd suddenly have a perfect marriage. Instead the next weeks were agonising.

James   I wouldn't wish for any husband to hear the things she told me. I figured she must be loaded with guilt, and that as long as this went on, we hadn't a prayer. The only thing I could work out to do was to dig it all out of her. So I elected myself her psychiatrist. We went on interminable automobile rides and I probed. In the end she told me everything – you never heard anything so lurid.

Barbara   For the first time in my life I was totally free – there was nothing buried, nothing to be afraid of any more. James didn't move out – but for six years we didn't communicate. He didn't even give me birthday or Christmas cards. Most of our friends dumped us – and that really hurt him.

James   Then I was asked to do the music for the film of a big musical, which was to be made in England. It was a tremendous challenge. We found a lovely house in London and I used the top floor as my office. I started a liaison with Liz, a brilliant lady who was also working on the film.

Barbara   When I first began to find a faith I was so self-righteous that James screamed at me, 'You have all the answers to everything!' But by the time we went to London I had stopped preaching at him. Every morning I made time to meditate and listen to the inner voice. We entertained a lot and I tried to do everything the way James wanted.
    One Sunday I took tea upstairs to James

'The door was open a crack and I could see James on his knees holding her.'

and Liz. As I got to the top floor I heard Liz sobbing. The door was open a crack and I could see her sitting on the couch and James on his knees holding her. As the teacups started to rattle I went downstairs and into my bathroom, where I used to go to pray. 'Lord what is going on?' I asked. 'I've done everything I thought was right.' A thought came back to me, loud and clear: 'Ask him. Don't point a finger and don't accuse him. Just ask him quietly.'

So I waited patiently until she left. I cooked a beautiful dinner, lit the candles and when we had finished eating I put my hand on his arm and said, 'Darling, is there something going on with you and Liz?'

James   I gave her an honest answer: 'Yes, there's plenty going on; I love her with all my heart. One of the main reasons is that laughter is an important part of my life and I've been married to you forever and I can't remember when we have laughed together. With her I've found out what laughter is again. Married to you I lost it.' I stormed out and went straight to Liz's apartment.

I came home at five the next morning and I gave Barbara an ultimatum: 'You can have me in this house if you want me – with no questions asked now that it's out in the open, and on one condition. Three nights a week I'm with her. You can have the other four. Take it or leave it.'

Barbara   I agreed. I knew that if I refused he would walk out, divorce me and marry her. For by this time, having got rid of the guilt and fears, I had begun to learn what love was all about. I loved him more than I ever thought possible. I began to pray for a sense of humour.

We lived like that for 13 months. It was

terribly difficult. I would go to my friends and scream and cry. Each of our children came over at separate times to see England, each with terrible problems, still not having forgiven us.

That's when I began to love God, because He gave me the strength and grace to go through all this. And I began to be able to laugh and to see the fun in James, which I had shut out for so long.

James   I came home once and she was dressing to go out with me, hair in curlers. I had begun to be aware that for some inexplicable, crazy, cooky reason this woman loved me. What made it so unfathomable to me was that I couldn't stand me. I had been such a stinker. Why did she love me? I asked her outright why she wanted to stay with me. She talked for five to seven minutes, like the flow of a brook, so beautifully and with no hesitation. 'Who could be the no-good that I've been and be idiot enough to walk away from a love like that?' I asked myself.

Barbara   The only trouble was that he didn't tell me this. I was hanging on by my eyelids – we were due to leave England in several weeks and I didn't know if he was going to stay and marry her or come home with me.

James   I knew I would never leave Barbara after that talk. But I was guilt-ridden about Liz: I had built up her hopes of a future together. I felt like a criminal who wanted to put the money back in the bank before he was caught. At one point I even thought fleetingly, 'There's one way out of this – to do away with myself.' That's how tortured I was. But in the end I did break with Liz.

Barbara and I took a Mediterranean cruise.

The film opened in London and it was a smash hit. But it no longer mattered to me. All I wanted was to have time with Barbara. We did nothing but two-way talk. For the first time in our married life we had real communication.

Incidentally, I have discovered that Barbara has a delicious, quiet sense of humour. I'm a musician, I live by my ears. Her laughter is without any question the single most beautiful sound on earth to me.

Barbara   In time our children came to forgive us. It took our youngest daughter 17 years – but it was the greatest gift I've ever had when she finally did.

Chapter 4

Going it alone

Since the 1970s, the number of single-parent families in the Canadian province of Quebec has nearly doubled. In Britain, where numbers have also soared, one family in seven is now headed by a single parent.

How do single parents cope with the daunting task of bringing up their families alone? And what about loneliness? And how can those who have suffered avoid poisoning their children with blame and bitterness?

Battered wife

Lucy, a senior neuro-surgical sister from Soweto, has had to face up to all these questions. She lives with her teenage son, Eric, in North London. She met her husband, Bob, who is also South African, in London. She writes:

We were very happy together in the beginning. Bob did his full share in the house and with our baby boy, Eric. His business was doing well and we decided together that I should carry on nursing so that we could save for a house of our own.

Then things began to go wrong – Bob was getting irritable. He even started knocking me about. I asked him what the matter was. He said it was just the pressure of his business. I suggested giving up my job so that I could have more time at home, but he wouldn't hear of it. Then a girl from our own country whom we had befriended told me she was having an affair with Bob. I had never suspected it. I rushed home, burnt my wedding dress and packed my bags.

Bob begged me to give him another chance

Margaret Gray

43

and I agreed for Eric's sake. For a time all went well. Then the violence started again. I had to go to hospital five times – once he nearly blinded me.

He kept saying he was sorry and asking for another chance, but then I found he had spent our savings on other women – and I also felt in danger of my life. I was determined my son shouldn't suffer any more scenes, so I took him and went into hiding for a time. I was bitter and lost and I didn't know which way to turn.

I ended up in a hostel for the homeless. There I met a young white woman with illegitimate twins. She had left home when she was 16 because her mother 'didn't understand' her and she had had the twins on her 17th birthday. She never spoke to any of us in the hostel and was always shouting at the twins, who cried all night. This made her more irritable and the other mothers, who were being kept awake, became aggressive towards her.

One night when I was exhausted after my ward work I realised that there wasn't the usual noise coming from the girl's room. I took my courage in my hands and knocked on the door. She opened it looking weak and ill. I offered her some milk and tried to cheer her up. In the end she told me she missed her home and couldn't cope. I suggested she talk to her mother, but she said, 'My mother never wanted to hear about my problems. She said I was too young to have any. We never really talked as mother and daughter. *Her* problems came first and last.'

In the morning she knocked on my door. She brought 20 sleeping tablets which she said she would have taken the night before if I hadn't dropped in. She gave me a piece of paper with a phone number on it and said,

'Here, please yourself, that's my mother's phone number. Don't say I didn't warn you.'

During my lunch-break that day I put in a call to the number and that was the beginning of a new life for them all. The twins' grandmother came and took the children, and later they came to London to see us. My son said, 'Look Mum, the twins are smiling.'

Eric was nine then. We learnt how to be really honest with each other. We discussed his problems at school and which school he should go to and I told him all I felt about my marriage. At one point I asked him, 'Do you blame me in any way for the break-up?' He said, 'No.' If he had blamed me, I would have tried again to make a go of it.

Eric was visiting Bob at weekends. In my heart I wanted him to hate his father. 'Why do you tell me to love Dad, and then say horrible things about him?' he asked me one day. I realised I was destroying Eric with my hatred and I started to pray every day that God would take my bitterness away. He has, but I still have to pray about it every day. I said to Eric, 'We must love the good in your father and leave the bad,' and I stopped trying to poison his mind.

Sometimes I found that when I had a frown on my face, looking at Eric's old school shoes or pyjamas and wondering how to buy new ones, all he really needed from me was a hug and to hear me say, 'I love you'. As I struggled to get the breakfast ready on time, all he wanted was for me to talk to him. He felt secure in my love for him. His headmistress once said to me, 'I would never have dreamt that your son comes from a divided home – he is one of the most secure and outgoing children in the school.'

At the beginning, my job saved my reason, because my patients took my whole attention.

From the time I arrived at the hospital until I left I could forget about my own problems. When I look at some of my patients I feel that although I have suffered there are people who are far worse off than I am.

The other day a patient came in with a cerebral tumour. I went into his room to see him, and asked him for his next-of-kin's address so that I could obtain consent for his surgery. He told me that he was divorced, had no family and didn't want anyone to know about his operation. He asked me if I had a family in Britain and I explained I had; he broke down and told me how alone he was. I insisted that he give me his ex-wife's phone number.

Although we are not supposed to go against the patient's wishes, I phoned his ex-wife. She decided to come and see him – a difficult decision as they had not been in touch for years. She brought their two children. They continued to visit him after that and I think they began to be a family once again.

Car crash   **Soon after they married, David and Gillian emigrated to Southern Rhodesia (now Zimbabwe). They built their own house, had two children and, once Gillian had got over her homesickness, planned to spend their lives there. At the same time they each began to find a faith which gave fresh purpose and meaning to their lives.**

Then, eight years after they got married, tragedy struck. Gillian was 28. She says:

We were driving home from South Africa, laughing and talking like a couple of children. We were so happy because we had just been at a conference where we had found something special – a really firm joint commitment to put God first in our lives and try to do what He asked us to. We felt more united than we had ever done before.

Suddenly as we crossed a low-level bridge our car bounced off the tarmac strips in the middle of the dirt road. It fell about 20 feet. I had just unlocked my door – something I never normally did in a car – and it flew open and I was thrown out. I rolled over and over like a football, repeating, 'I'm going to die; I'm going to die.' As I landed in a thornbush it seemed as if two huge Gothic doors were closing in front of me, and I knew I would live.

I was stuck in the bush, screaming. It was just as if someone slapped me in the face and I stopped. Then I began to get instructions, 'Move your left leg' and so on. I followed them and managed to get free. 'I must find David,' I thought; but someone – I felt it was God – said, 'He's not there.' As I looked at the car, it's hard to explain, but I saw David's spirit leave it. I knew it was him – and I wanted him to go, because where he was going seemed so marvellous, and yet I wanted him to stay. When I made it to the car, I saw he was dead.

As I sat by the deserted road, waiting for a car to pass, I stormed at God, 'You've given us everything this weekend with one hand and taken it away with the other.'

'All I've done is taken David,' came the answer. 'You've still got the unity I've given you.'

When I eventually got home, I had to decide what to tell Matthew, who was then five. In the end I told him about the doors – how David had gone through them, but I had had to stay behind. 'Why didn't they let you through, Mummy?' he asked. I said I didn't know. 'I think it's because Jesus wants you to be an old lady,' he said and went out to play. Next day he told me, 'My Daddy's in a lovely golden-white place.'

Eighteen months later we went home to Britain. We'd only been back for about 6 months when Matthew got meningitis. He was in a coma for a fortnight. Once again I was furious with God. 'You've taken one,' I said. 'You're not going to take another.' In a quiet way, God answered back, 'Matthew belongs to me and not to you. I'll decide whether he lives or dies.' I knew I had to say, 'OK – then you can have him.'

Then I went to the hospital. I found Matthew sitting up and saying, 'Hello, Mummy.' The illness had been caused by a growth at the base of his brain and the middle ear. We had come home just in time – it couldn't have been operated on in Southern Africa.

However well-meaning friends are at times like these, it's not the same as having another parent. And the little things are often worst – I used to find it so hard to go to activities at the children's schools on my own. In some ways, too, it's easier to cope alone when the children are young than it is when the emotional problems start in their teens. I'm sorry now that I didn't give them more time – especially my daughter, Kate.

When Kate was 17 she fell for someone who got her on to drugs. It was only soft drugs, thank heavens – but she used to disappear for weeks at a time. I'd have no clue where she was. I used to phone every number I had. This went on for a couple of years. Then late one night the police called to say they had picked her up. I went to the police station and there she was – out for the count on the cell floor, like a bundle of rags. She was hardly recognisable. I got her home and into court next day, where she was fined £2.

I was really desperate. Matthew had been

'There she was – out for the count on the cell floor, like a bundle of rags.'

abroad for some months, so he didn't know how bad things were.

I rang a friend connected with a rehabilitation centre for hard addicts. He suggested we sleep on the problem. Next morning he told me he thought the answer would come through the family. Meanwhile the only idea I had had was that I should get in touch with Matthew – who I knew was working on a yacht in a marina in Palma in Majorca. I had the yacht's name, but I wasn't certain the telegram would find him. He rang right away. 'Get her out here and I'll look after her,' he said. He was too generous to tell me that he had no money.

Right up to the day before her flight I didn't know if she would go. On the last day we went shopping for her clothes. She didn't

49

seem in the least interested – and I was praying hard. Suddenly – from one side of the road to the other – she changed. She got excited about the trip and started looking forward to seeing Matthew. She spent her last evening with her cousin who was dying of cancer. It was the first time for ages she had wanted to do something for someone else.

She was away for five months, cooking and looking after children on the yacht where Matthew was working as a sailor. It gave her the break she needed. Then I got a card saying they were coming home. My heart filled with fear.

When she got back all her old friends started ringing up again. One day she and her boyfriend were having a row and I realised she was on the fringe of the drug circle again. I was afraid they would get violent – so I called Matthew, who was upstairs recovering from a cartilage operation. 'Why is it so impossible for you to get a job?' I burst out at her. 'Oh, Mum, but I'm two months pregnant,' she said. Matthew and I just looked at each other.

She came back from the doctor next day and told me the options – abortion, adoption, or keeping the baby. 'It's your decision,' I said. I felt wretched having to be so hard, but I knew I shouldn't tell her what to do. One morning she phoned me at work and told me that she'd realised that if she had an abortion she'd never again take responsibility for anything.

She decided to keep the baby and the family rallied round with gifts. She got a job until just before the baby was born. Her son's arrival really changed her life; she became so responsible. The baby's father wanted her to move in with him – there was no thought of marriage – but she decided to go it alone. When her son was about two and a half, she married someone else and they now have two more children.

I used to get this longing – 'Oh God, David, why aren't you here?' But the way God has used each tragedy has made me richer. And that takes away a lot of the hurt. I would have loved to have married again, but I have found I don't need a husband to lead a fulfilling life.

Cut in half

At the age of 39 Margaret found herself alone with four children aged from two to 16. Being divorced, she says, was like being 'cut in half'. She goes on:

My husband had been asking for a divorce for ten years but I had not agreed. Eventually he took us away on holiday to the same camp site where he had taken his mistress six weeks before. The first night someone recognised him from his previous visit. I felt, 'If he can do this, there's nothing left.' I found that because of his persistent unfaithfulness I no longer trusted him.

A friend said, 'This has been an aching tooth for too long – isn't it time it came out?'

This was a shock. I had to think long and hard what was right for him, the children and me. I prayed about it, too. Finally I knew I must make a clean break and divorce him. The children and I then left London for a new home in the country.

My father died when I was a baby. I had to leave school when I was only 14 because my mother could not afford my uniform. When Mike and I married we didn't have much, but in time we had built up to a nice home and two cars. Now things became very difficult economically again.

Three years after we moved into our new

home, a man arrived on my doorstep with a summons. Mike hadn't been paying the mortgage. We were living on social security and we couldn't pay, so we were turned out. We found a run-down house in the village and paid rent for it until our old house sold and we could buy it. It took another three years. Meanwhile we had so little that I couldn't even pay for the removals van.

The lease said I had to put a fence up – along a terrific length of garden. I didn't know how I'd pay for it, but as soon as we moved in the man next door asked if I minded if he put up a fence. A little later he came round and said that he and his wife were going out for the day and could they take my four-year-old, Tim. They were childless and from then on they half-adopted him – helping with his clothes and his school fees when he went to an assisted boarding school, and visiting him there when I could not afford to. They were marvellous to him – but they never overstepped the mark or tried to take my place.

We went through the most terrible times. Often Mike didn't pay the maintenance and I'd have to take him to court. I never knew if he would pay next month. I can remember only having 10p at one point – then a neighbour turned up with £5, which she said she wanted to give me. We used to find cauliflowers on the doorstep. We seldom had any money, but God looked after us.

At first I was bitter and resentful – and at the same time I hoped our marriage might be remade. But after a while my husband remarried. I found this very hard to bear. I had to overcome the humiliation of rejection and give up all hope of reconciliation. Eventually, after eight years, the wound healed. Today we are friends again. We go to family gatherings and consult each other on family matters.

With the four children, the house and garden, different part-time jobs and the Young Wives' Group at the local church to run, I had no time to sit around and I quickly made new friends. I often longed to remarry – but, as I did not want to replace the children's father while they were still at home, I put this off until later. After all my own mother, after some very hard years, had remarried happily when she was 50.

But it didn't happen. By the time I was 50 the three eldest children had married and Tim was at boarding school. I suddenly felt I was no longer needed. I became depressed, partly due to the side-effects of pills I was taking for high blood pressure. I'd just got a full-time job, but I didn't want to go on fighting. 'Oh Lord, why don't you let me die now?' I even asked.

I had been a Christian for 20 years and felt that I had a strong faith. So why should I feel like this? What about all the things I had planned to do when the children had gone? How often I had longed to be able to read undisturbed, to have a peaceful meal, to listen to my kind of music, travel to other countries. . . It gradually dawned on me that I had been living for the future. When my dreams didn't materialise, I was downcast. I kept going, but I felt stale and stuck in a rut.

Then one Sunday, I went to a Christian Fellowship in our town. It was a shock – there were lots of young people and children, singing and chatting and dancing. There was a tremendous freedom as well as great depth in the teaching. I felt Jesus was there. I began to get involved and found that I could share all the things I had learnt over the years – and be myself.

I realised that I hadn't let God into every room in my heart – I had kept my future for myself. I began to see that the terrible emptiness I felt must be filled with God's Holy Spirit. It took some time for this to happen, but when it did, joy, love, peace and hope began to flow back into my life again. I understand now that I am meant to be a channel for God to work through – and that that, not my plans and hopes for the future, is what matters.

Since I've had this deeper relationship with Christ, a whole new dimension of life has opened up for me. I feel needed again in a different way. A friend in the village said the other day, 'It's really nice to see Margaret fulfilled.' And it's true. I've just retired from my job, but I'm so happy.

Chapter 5

Trying again

**Three-quarters of the British people who get divorced remarry –
half of them within five years. In the early 70s these marriages
were more likely to succeed than the ones they replaced, but now
the figures have changed. 40% of second marriages now end in
divorce, as against 30% of first marriages.**

**How can people who decide to give marriage a second try
avoid making the same mistakes again?**

Spider's web

Moira is a lawyer. She lives in a big American city with her second husband, Jack, their two small daughters and her son from her first marriage. She describes how she escaped from the prison of the past:

When I left my first husband I was terribly afraid, hurt and angry. I jumped to the nearest person or job; I couldn't wait; I couldn't be alone. Why should this happen to me, I asked myself angrily. I wasn't very good, but did I deserve all this? I was stuck with a small child, no money, no family. It wasn't my fault and it wasn't fair that people should look down on me. I felt as if I had lost everything I had ever had and everything I had ever expected. I refused the help people offered, because I wanted to feel in control.

But there were people who loved me in spite of everything. Time passed, healing set in and I remarried.

One afternoon, as I was sitting outdoors on a balcony, I saw a small spider in the middle of its web on the railing. As I watched, I realised that my life had been like a spider's. I was the centre of my world and from my

Eric and David Hosking

web I had lured people to me and used them. I had only thought of people in terms of what they could do for me.

Then another thought struck me – 'God made that spider and He loves it. God made me also; He loves me.' I saw that I had to unravel the web of self-deceit I had woven around myself. It was destructive – and unnecessary.

I began with Jack, my new husband. Slowly, sometimes painfully, I began to tell him about all the lies and half-truths I had told. When at last I had corrected all the deceptions I could remember, I felt free. There was no longer any need for a protective barrier between us. Although it was painful for both of us, we built a strong foundation for our marriage.

I began to see why I had married my first husband. I wanted to get away from home; other people thought it was a good idea; I wanted to be supported while I studied music; I had been in love with someone else and thought I would never love anyone again, so it didn't matter who I married. My first husband wanted to marry me very much and I think in his own way loved me. I was angry when it did not turn out the way I expected.

As I realised my side of it all, I felt truly sorry. Although he had started out with a fine education and with money and family advantages, he was now serving a prison term for using his clients' funds for his own purposes. He had lost his business and his freedom and a great deal more. I asked myself, 'If I did care for him, if he was important to me, what would I do?'

I decided that one thing I could do was to give him back some jewellery he had given me while we were married. He could use it as a nest-egg to begin his life again when he was released from prison. At one time I had thought, 'Over my dead body will he get anything from me.' He had spent huge sums on luxuries, paid nothing for the support of our child and made my life as tough as possible. It felt strange to go against the grain of feelings I had had for years.

I wrote to him to apologise for my part in the breakdown of our marriage. He replied, 'I was simply overwhelmed by the kindness you expressed. I cried all evening. My life these past years has been nothing but bitter experiences, which makes your generosity and kindness all the more wonderful.' The past no longer poisons the present.

A couple of years ago I had a big opportunity. I had been working in our state legislature for ten years. Then my candidate was elected mayor of our city. I had paid my dues, done the staff work and it was my turn. I could write my own ticket and be one of the top members of his staff.

I loved working in government, but I often felt torn between my family and my job. Jack was a frantically busy doctor, and we had just had our first daughter. After a real struggle I decided that although my chance might never come again, this wasn't the right time for me to take it. The important thing was to hold my new marriage and my family together.

In a strange way, when I gave up my fondest ambition, it came back to me, and I didn't have to sacrifice my family. Recently I had an idea about how the mayor could help some of the poorest people in our city. I wrote a proposal and gave it to him as a private citizen. He asked me to run the programme for him and I am now doing so.

Vital 'but' 'Would you like to marry a divorced man?' Klaus asked Sigrid as they walked in the

59

'Would you like to marry a divorced man?' Klaus asked Sigrid.

Swiss mountains. She accepted. 'What encourages me most,' she says after two and a half years of marriage, 'is that someone who has been so deeply hurt could find the faith to put his trust in another person again.'

Klaus was away on a business trip when his first wife, Hilde, decided to leave him. When he returned to their flat in Germany, she was gone. 'I tried to get her to come back, but she refused,' he says. 'She had found someone who did not have to travel as much as I did. She had always blamed me for the times she was alone.'

German law requires a two-year separation before a divorce can be granted. 'For the first months I felt such a failure that I cut off all my links with other people,' Klaus continues. 'If anyone at work asked after Hilde, I found it very difficult to admit she was no longer with me. Then there was a brief stage when I said to myself, "I'm free again, I can do whatever I like!" It didn't last long. I knew that somehow I had to get my life streamlined again.' Slowly he began to reopen his communication lines, appreciating those friends who were willing to stand by him without demanding a closer relationship than he felt able to give.

Then came the divorce case, with the legal decisions about property and alimony, somewhat simplified by the fact that Klaus and Hilde had no children. 'Our judge wouldn't allow the case to disintegrate into a bazaar,' says Klaus. 'So often a divorce settlement can destroy the future of a second marriage before it even begins. I have colleagues who have had to sell their homes and cars and send most of their income to their first wives. How can a second wife accept that?' He was allowed to pay alimony in a lump sum.

Now Klaus had the financial freedom to

think about remarriage, and there were business incentives as well. 'People in management tend to feel that if you're not married, you're not reliable enough to handle difficult cases, because you have no stability at home. So although I was investing a lot of time in my career, nothing was coming of it.' At the same time, when a friend suggested he should remarry he was upset. 'You can't just say, "It wasn't fair, let's try again!" You need time to think out what went wrong,' he says.

'When your marriage breaks down, you start out by blaming the other person,' he goes on. 'But then you begin to think, "OK, she had her problems, but. . . " That "but" is very important for any new relationship – it's how you realise where you were wrong. Often it's the smaller items of married life, not the big ones. . . and the inability to clear the atmosphere after disagreements.'

Klaus and Hilde had married in church, and this worried him. What about the promise to stay together 'until death us do part'? It hadn't been Klaus who broke the promise – but was he really free? Could he say to God, 'You know better than I what went wrong, but I'd like to try to promise again'? Different friends gave him different answers. 'In the end I suddenly felt that this was not something God was unwilling to forgive,' he says. 'This gave me peace.'

Sigrid had, in a way, been prepared for his proposal by a previous love affair. She reckoned it was no thanks to herself that she had not ended up marrying the wrong man. 'God picked me up by the scruff of my neck and stopped things going too far,' she says. 'So who was I to refuse someone whom God had allowed to make a mistake, so as to help him through it?'

They started out on a basis of complete

openness about the past, trusting each other enough to talk about everything. 'I had to be willing to go through the pain Klaus had suffered,' says Sigrid. 'I came to the point when I hated his first wife. Then I had a surprising thought – that perhaps I should be grateful to her, because without her, we wouldn't have met.'

Klaus's work still takes him away for more of the year than he is at home. 'But now I tell Sigrid how sorry I am to go and we do a lot more to keep in touch,' he says. They write to each other nearly every day when they are apart. They phone whenever they can, and every three months set aside a weekend together with no interruptions.

'I accepted before we got married that it was going to be normal for us to be apart,' says Sigrid. 'I see our times together as a special gift, rather than something I'm entitled to and this means I can enjoy them to the full, instead of nagging him about why he can't stay longer or dreading the next parting. Of course, I have to decide this again and again.' She also decided, in spite of being a 'very fearful person', not to worry about his safety when he was travelling or to doubt his faithfulness to her while he was away. She has a demanding job of her own, and this helps too. 'It means I don't have to rely on Klaus for recognition and satisfaction.'

On his side, Klaus has decided to switch off the stresses of his working day before he comes home, rather than taking them out on his wife – another change from the past. 'Some days I do better than others,' he admits, 'but I pray about it. And I feel free to tell Sigrid as I come through the door if I need extra time to sort things out before we start talking.'

'We were clear when we fell in love that

this relationship would only work if it was based not just on our promise but on a daily turning back to the faith that God wants us together,' says Klaus. 'I now feel I can talk about my divorce with my colleagues. As a result, they often tell me their problems. We don't go into details, but I am able to tell them that a new beginning is possible.'

Second time lucky?

It is a fallacy to believe you can build a new, happy relationship on the unresolved blame and bitterness of a first marriage. 'The same person who created problems in the former marriage will be part of the new one,' comments one of my American friends who has been through this experience.

'When I got married for the second time,' she goes on, 'I brought with me the same patterns which helped to break up my first marriage; but I was not aware of it. My trouble was that I always played the victim; it was an automatic response. Only recently I discovered it only takes one of us to stop this destructive game. Then the other one has no one left to play with. When I decided to stop being the doormat and to start telling the truth, I became free. It was the beginning of a totally different relationship.'

Extended families

A tenth of all American children, according to a 1982 Census Bureau study, live with one step-parent and one birth parent. Combining two families has its problems, as another of my friends has found. Angela has three children from her first marriage. 'When I broke up with my first husband, I didn't realise how much I would miss the partnership of being parents,' she says. 'Even if you don't agree on everything to do with their upbringing, you still share deeply the concern when the children are sick or the pride when they come home with a good report card.

'My second husband has an eleven-year-old daughter. I can't help feeling differently towards her than I do towards my own – and it's the same for my husband, only the other way round. I often feel torn between my own daughter who wants to watch her favourite TV show on one channel and my husband who wants to watch the baseball. Somehow, when step-parents and stepchildren are involved, the issues which arise in any family become more complicated.

'A second marriage is no easier than the first one. New factors come into play and you bring with you all the garbage of the first marriage as well. I sometimes wonder whether we wouldn't work harder at the first marriage if we realised earlier what a break-up and new marriage involved. And I haven't mentioned all the agony the children have to go through . . .'

In spite – or because – of all this, Angela and her new husband are determined to make a success of this marriage. They now have a baby son, whom, says Angela, 'we all adore'.

Child's eye view

A few years ago we were invited to lunch by an elderly couple. They were overjoyed because their daughter, divorced for eight years, had just remarried her former husband. They were particularly delighted because of the effect on their three grandchildren, whom they had been looking after while their parents were apart.

One in five British children see their parents divorce before they are 16. For some the experience is more traumatic than others – but contrary to common assumptions, recent research has shown that children are more damaged by divorce than they are by the arguments and atmosphere

of an unhappy marriage. Even the most civilised divorce can leave lasting scars on the children – as Edward, now a father himself, has found out:

My parents drifted into divorce through separation. My father was working in the Far East. When I was 12 my parents brought me to Britain for major surgery. After my convalescence my father had to return to his work, while my mother stayed in Britain with me.

One day my mother called me into the living-room. She sounded rather brusque and I wondered what I had done. She was sitting on a camphor-wood chest, her back to the window, knitting.

'Daddy and I have decided to get divorced,' she said in a business-like way. It was almost a passing remark among the rows of stitches, but it set off an explosion in my heart. I swore, shouted and stamped at her. Then shame and terrible pain brimmed in. I fled, to sob myself dry on my bed. After that, no more tears, no feelings, just the ache.

Both my parents remarried in time. I grew up and studied. I felt I had been lucky – there had been no fighting or bitterness that I had been aware of and I liked both my step-parents. The break-up of my family had left me unscarred, after the first shock. When I married at thirty, both sets of parents were at the wedding. It was all very adult and civilised.

One morning, in reply to my half-yearly letter, I received two letters, one from my mother and one from my stepfather. 'I have taken all I can,' wrote my mother. 'I never want anything to do with you again.' My stepfather wrote, 'I will thank you not to write to my wife in the future.' I was dumbfounded. Whatever was this about? My

'It was almost a passing remark among the rows of stitches, but it set off an explosion in my heart.'

relationship with my mother had never been very close, but that was hardly grounds for such vehement rejection. Vainly I tried to recall the contents of my last letter.

There had to be good reasons – a mother does not write off an only child for nothing. I had recently become a Christian, committed to striving for a better world. If I couldn't be in harmony with those I professed to love, it made no sense to expect I could do better with the world at large. So instead of self-righteously washing my hands and blaming my mother, I prayed for some insight and guidance as to why these letters had been written. It took a long time to come.

Eventually one morning in the quiet following prayer, thoughts came tumbling out. I filled 12 pages of a notebook with them.

They went back to that fateful talk in the living-room. I saw now that my mother's brusque manner had been not heartlessness, but the result of her effort to control her own fears and pain. I had never before recognised the situation as difficult for *her*.

I also saw myself – a 13-year-old struggling with a hurricane of feelings. My world had been devastated. Everything was adrift, and unconsciously I had sought for a pattern that would make sense of the pieces. I was being hurt. Mother had been the cause. Father had been hurt by Mother as well, therefore he and I were allies. I had found a scapegoat for my pain and a focus for my loyalty and love.

From then on I lived with my mother like a parasite – taking her love and care, a home, food, pocket money, holidays, presents and giving very little in return. My father, I thought, was altogether superior and I modelled myself on the image I had of him. I was self-centred, off-hand, arrogant, rude and demanding.

Suddenly I saw the effects a 'good divorce' had had on me. It had stunted my emotional and social development and affected every relationship I had had from then on. I had been run by my 13-year-old values and attitudes for years; growing older without maturing.

It took a while for all this to sink in. As it did, I felt ashamed. I wrote to both my mother and stepfather asking their forgiveness, point by point, for every wrong I had done them over 25 years. It was a long letter, to which I did not expect a reply.

But a reply came, by return of post, full of

forgiveness and repentance for other incidents. When we met later we sat in the sun and opened our hearts to each other. We wept for our lost years. There is a new relationship between us now, although old weeds still occasionally grow and have to be uprooted. It is still not easy.

Facing the truth about myself and asking forgiveness retrieved a hopeless situation. It has enabled me to understand myself and others better and strengthened my faith in God, and my belief that repentance and forgiveness are crucial elements in fruitful human relationships. But even now I find it hard to tolerate someone talking to me when they are knitting.

Chapter 6

What price freedom?

'In dealing with couples in conflict, the real problems are often not between them but in each of the partners themselves,' writes Paul Tournier in *Escape from Loneliness*, (Highland Books, 1983). 'If each is set free by an inner experience, no marital problem is left, even if their differences of taste and ideas, which seem to divide them, remain.'

What does it mean to be really free? Is it possible – or do we always have to be enslaved by someone or something?

Sex

For many couples, sex is an area of conflict. Often the husband wants more of it, while the wife wants a good night's sleep.

Of course sex is also a bond. The trouble starts, as Roger and Debbie found out, when it becomes the only bond.

Roger and Debbie met in Sheffield, England, just as Debbie was coming to the end of her secretarial course at college and Roger was winding up a research project at the University. 'It's fair to say it was love at first sight,' says Roger. 'I was recovering from a serious bout of depression resulting from the breakdown of a previous relationship. Debbie blew into my life like a breath of fresh air. We were soon going out regularly to parties and night-clubs and we were sleeping together long before we could really claim to know each other.'

Debbie's childhood had been tough. Her mother had been divorced when Debbie was only a few months old and the resulting remarriage was unhappy. She had been physically abused by her stepfather and the responsibility for bringing up her younger brother and sister was thrust upon her. In her teens she had suffered from anorexia – very seriously at one point – and had turned to boys for the love and attention she did not receive at home. Her relationship with Roger, she felt, was the best thing that had ever happened to her.

Roger felt the same way. They had little prospect of finding jobs in Sheffield, so they planned to go to London. For the sake of convenience, they decided to live together. 'Growing up in the wake of the swinging 60s, it was always one of my ambitions to live with my girl-friend,' says Roger. 'It was a stage in my development I thought I ought to pass through.

'Setting up a home together in London was exciting. We had all the fun of having one another, employment and no real responsibilities. But sex was the only thing holding us together. The more we indulged, the less exciting it became and the less interest we took in one another.'

'I was totally dependent on Roger and terrified to let go of him,' says Debbie. Neither of them would have admitted to each other, or to anyone else, that the relationship was going down the drain. 'You both realise that the slightest thing may upset the apple cart and end the whole thing, so there's no room for honesty,' remembers Roger. 'Sordid though it becomes, you hold on to what you have.'

They planned to be married, but Roger called it off at the last minute. The climax was a disastrous holiday in Portugal. Two weeks of sex, sun-bathing and cheap wine did nothing to improve things. Roger was already on the look-out for someone new.

When they got back to London, an acquaintance got in touch with Roger. They had first met on a bus the year before, when this man had told Roger about his belief that a new society must be based on change in people's attitudes and behaviour. He had spoken about his vision of what the world would be like if people put God first in their lives. And he had illustrated it with stories of how people who had put their personal lives in order had influenced world events. As a socialist and active trade unionist, Roger had been impressed. They had exchanged addresses and Roger hadn't thought much more about it.

Now this man was visiting London and Roger took Debbie along to meet him. He suggested to them that if they wanted to be effective forces for change in the world, they should look at the way they were living themselves. The afternoon ended with a few moments of quiet reflection.

'I recognised that my whole philosophy in life was to change other people and not myself,' says Roger. Debbie saw how bitter she was towards her family – but what amazed her most was that Roger should be so honest about himself. They decided to make an experiment – to see what happened if they tried to live by absolute standards of morality and took time each day to reflect quietly on their lives and what to do.

Roger embarked on a period of intensive activity, putting right things which he felt were wrong in his life. 'I opened up with Debbie about relationships I had not told her about. I had been dishonest with money – cheating the Department of Health and Social Security, for example. This money had to be repaid. And I owned up to two professors about misrepresenting some research results, which had been published. As I found the strength to do these things, I began to find a faith in God – I knew I could never have done them on my own.'

Meanwhile Debbie began to see where she had gone wrong with her parents. 'It didn't matter what they had done to me; my secrecy and hatred were wrong,' she said. Encouraged by the change in Roger, she started to put things right herself. 'We found something completely new for our relationship.' She apologised to her parents – and so did Roger, for 'taking their daughter away from them, without ever stopping to think about what they were feeling'. He put things right with his own parents too.

As the experiment progressed, both began to feel that their relationship could be permanent – 'that God had a plan for our lives, together'. They decided to get married. 'We didn't go through the ceremony simply to get a certificate,' says Roger. 'Marrying just for the sake of respectability is no better than living together – the relationship is just as liable to get off on the wrong foot. We were married in order to make a public commitment before our friends, our family and God. We really meant it when we said "as long as we both on earth shall live".'

The most revolutionary change in their lifestyle now was accepting a target of absolute purity, drawn, Roger says, from the New Testament. 'To a left-wing socialist like myself any talk of sexual morality was anathema,' he says. 'I'm an anarchist by instinct – I can't abide rules. But purity freed us from exploiting each other and from the bondage of constantly trying to please senses which had been neutralised by over-indulgence.'

'This was real liberation for me,' says

Debbie. 'We had tried every form of contraception available. All were unpleasant and some made me quite ill. When we chose self-discipline, the need for any sort of contraception vanished and along with it a whole host of worries about side-effects and effectiveness.' Purity, they say, doesn't mean an end to sex, but that they are no longer controlled by it.

They now have two children. 'I don't believe that it's possible to build an unselfish, caring and equal society if you are a dictator and exploiter in your own house,' says Roger. 'Honesty has revolutionised our relationship and laid a firm foundation for our marriage. When you've told each other about the most shameful things from the past, you have nothing left to throw at each other. So many people are bottled up by the fear of being found out.'

Drastic remedy

Others have different tyrants to fight.

Ruth and Bill live in California. Their quarrels were tearing their marriage apart. Eventually Ruth traced the problem to its source – the cocktail hour. 'I wonder how many other relationships get spiked when each person chooses his or her verbal weapons after the first drink?' she asks. They didn't drink every day and she knew she wasn't an addict, but she decided to accept a drastic solution.

'The first party we went to after I gave up drink was a very happy one for me – to my amazement,' she says. 'I was brim-full of joy instead of being the quiet sobersides I'd expected to be. I knew I was on the right track and began to gain confidence.' Disagreements still arise – but she finds she can say what she feels in a relaxed and unemotional way, and encourage Bill rather than carping at him when things go wrong.

For George and Marion, who live in a large British city, the problem was more serious. George lost his job as a factory manager because of his alcoholism. They tell their own story:

George

I started drinking when I was in the Navy, not continuously at first, but very heavily when we went ashore. Later on I picked up the habit again from my father-in-law – he could down eight pints in one evening and go off to work next morning quite clear-headed.

I wasn't like that. These sessions left me completely blotto and the more I had, the more I wanted. It gradually got worse and I couldn't work for weeks on end. Not many people knew, outside the family – I even kidded myself that my wife and the two children didn't know. I managed to get the doctor to sign certificates saying I was unfit for work because of nervous trouble. At one time I could only get through the day if I laced my morning tea with a third of a cupful of vodka and put in plenty of sugar to disguise the taste.

Marion

You lose all trust when you live with an alcoholic. George would often swear to me that he was going to work and I knew he was going straight out to buy drink. Once I said, 'If you don't go to work today I won't be here when you get back,' and he knew I meant it. Several times I nearly left him, but I always stayed for the sake of the children.

He wasn't violent; he didn't even walk as if he was drunk; but he was intensely irritable nearly all the time and there was hardly any communication between us. He insisted on driving the car and it was absolutely hair-raising. Once I made him stop and let me out so I could catch the bus home.

I had a job at an infants' school. I didn't earn much, but I settled the housekeeping bills and left George to pay the rest. It wasn't easy bringing up two children with all the expenses of the teenage years, but they understood what was going on and were a support.

George   Things came to a head the day I had promised to take our son to a football match. I had been decorating that morning and had felt the need for a glass of sherry to keep me going. This glass had led to several more and eventually to three whole bottles! When we got to the football ground I went for a pint of beer and passed out. My son had to get me home – bitterly disappointed at missing the match.

Marion insisted that I went to the doctor. Once again I lied, telling him I had had an attack of vertigo and once more he gave me some pills. Next day I did some more decorating and when Marion got home she found me with a cut in my forehead bleeding profusely. I had no recollection of having hurt myself. This time she insisted I tell the doctor the truth, and in a short time I found myself in a nerve hospital being dried out.

One day as I was sitting by myself I had a strange experience. I felt a presence with me and great strength pouring into me. I knew it was Jesus. He said to me, 'You are an alcoholic; it is a cross you will have to bear for life. You are to go out and help other alcoholics.' I went to find the doctor on duty and told him, 'I know that I am an alcoholic.' Up till then I had always insisted that it was

'You are an alcoholic; it is a cross you will have to bear for life.'

my nerves which made me drink. Now, the doctor told me, I could be cured.

From that day, seven years ago, I have not touched one drop of drink, nor have I craved for it. When the family cleared out the attic they found sackfuls of bottles. Being an alcoholic is hell, but my family suffered far more than I. I am so grateful for the way Marion stood by me all those years.

Now I am working full-time helping other people overcome their addiction, and this makes me really happy. We have a 99% success rate with the people who come to the clinic attached to our parish church. Recently I had a letter from a young woman who had heard me interviewed on the radio. Her marriage had broken up because of her drinking habits – but the interview had helped her to stop drinking and she was now reunited with her husband.

Three months to live

Ramesh and Sherna live in Bombay. Ramesh was a racehorse trainer and moved in fast-living circles, where he started taking drugs. Eventually Sherna had to face the fact that he was addicted – to the extent that the doctor gave him three months to live unless he stopped. Sherna wrote to me:

One day in desperation I asked God what to do. The answer came in the shape of a question, 'Do you love Ramesh enough for Me to use you to save his life?' After much thought I decided that I did.

That was in October. Before I could help Ramesh I knew I had to get myself straightened out. There were so many tensions in the home that we shared with my mother-in-law. She was a lady of strong feelings but she did not express them. I found that harder to deal with than if she had told me straight what she expected from me.

I realised that I was always putting Ramesh in third place – after his mother and myself – and trying to please everyone, which was impossible, of course. I was doing what I thought was expected of me, rather than what I felt deep down was right. I blamed my in-laws for encouraging Ramesh in his way of life.

I called a family conference with his mother, brothers and sisters. This took a lot of courage, but I felt it was our only hope. Every day we met together for a few minutes. Sparks flew in all directions. I apologised for whatever was true of the hurtful things my mother-in-law said to me and ignored the rest of her outbursts. This began to bring a new unity between us.

Ramesh used to ask for money, for the use of the car, for food and drink so that he could entertain his friends without me. He played different ones of the family against the others, so we needed a common strategy. We decided to say no to all requests. 'I know what you say is right,' my mother-in-law eventually told me. 'But I have never said no to Ramesh before and it is difficult to start now.'

We decided not to use force with Ramesh or tell him lies even for his own good. I tried not to react to his verbal attacks on me. It was rough going, but I did not allow myself to get into fights or arguments.

At Christmas we were invited to the hills by our cousins. They were delayed, so Ramesh, our two sons and I had the place to ourselves. While we were there Ramesh read a book which made a deep impression on him – the true story of a man who found a faith while lying badly injured in a prisoner-of-war hospital and of his escape to freedom, following directions from the inner voice.

After reading the book Ramesh decided

to stop taking drugs, smoking cigarettes and drinking alcohol. Later he threw all his liquor bottles and cigarettes into the dustbin. When we returned to Bombay he told his mother, 'This time I will not go back to the drugs, because this time God has freed me. So I feel no strain about maintaining my decision.'

The doctor had refused to treat him unless he really wanted to be cured. He now examined him. He was amazed that Ramesh had been able to give up his addictions so suddenly and totally, without experiencing any side-effects – no digestive ailments, brain damage or loss of muscle tone. It was a miracle.

Fear Most people have something they struggle to be free of, even if they are not addicts. For me it is fear.

When the Germans occupied Holland in 1940 they also occupied our house. I was six. For the next five years we lived in my grandparents' house. My dog and I were always the first in the shelter when the air-raid warning sounded. We would sit there together shaking until it was safe to go back to bed. We survived – but the house was so devastated in one raid that we had to move to my uncle and aunt's. After the war I hated fireworks because they sounded like bombs.

In 1943 my father was put into a hostage camp for five months. The next year he went into hiding and early one morning my mother was taken to a concentration camp because they could not find him. My grandmother was also arrested for a time. Thank God, they all came out alive.

A few years ago I decided to make a list of all the things I was most afraid of, to see if I could somehow become free of them. I realised that I was terrified of two things –

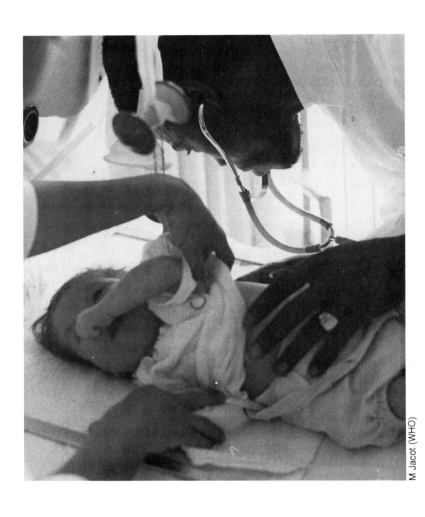

M Jacot (WHO)

'When Digna was five months old, one of the things I had always feared happened.' that I or someone I loved might land up in a concentration camp again or be tortured; or that Paul or one of the girls might be struck by some terrible accident or illness.

It was a relief to look these fears squarely in the face. When I told God about them it was as if He said to me, 'I am in control of your life. Even if any of these things do happen to you, I will be there with you and I will still be able to tell you what to do.'

When Digna, our younger daughter, was five months old, one of the things I had always feared happened. She became very ill and was rushed into hospital. She had to have an emergency operation for a bowel obstruction. During the operation Paul and I sat in a coffee shop a few streets away from the hospital. We felt so helpless. Deep down we knew that her life was in God's hands and that we had to trust that He knew what was best, whatever the outcome.

When we were allowed in to see her she was a pathetic sight – a tiny bundle in a big bed, with one tube in her nose and another in her arm. The doctor said she was going to be all right, but that it had been a very close call. At home we got on our knees to thank God for giving her back to us.

I know I have a choice – either to give in to fear or to trust, whether the crisis is a bumpy plane ride, a forthcoming public speech or a sleepless night wondering what a teenage daughter is up to.

Mother-in-law

Patricia lives in an idyllic setting, on the Californian coast looking out onto the Pacific. She and her husband have four sons – but their marriage nearly broke up because of her hatred of her mother-in-law.

'I was bitter because I felt my mother-in-law did not like me and wanted to break up our marriage,' she says. 'I would make disparaging remarks about her to my husband and the children which of course coloured their feelings for her.'

Eventually Patricia asked God to show her what to do about the relationship. She realised that she had been wrong in keeping her heart closed, whatever her mother-in-law's failings. 'I apologised. It wasn't easy and she wept. I realised how much she had wanted to be loved. When she wasn't, she had resorted to the negative. Getting our relationship straight brought a real understanding and love between us, which was reflected in the family. It brought peace in our home.'

Buried past

Every room in Greta's home is a work of art – curtains, lampshades, patchwork quilts all made by herself. She is married with two children, a warm-hearted and outgoing person, who had blocked out her unhappy childhood because it was too painful to face.

She had always been puzzled by the lack of affection she had received from her parents. Recently, when she was rummaging through an old box of papers in the attic, she found some family letters which explained everything. She discovered that she was not the child of her 'parents', but of her 'father's' unmarried sister. Her uncle and aunt had taken her in when she was five months old. She goes on:

I had always thought I couldn't remember anything of my childhood, but now it is beginning to come back to me without the pain which made me bury it. There is a real feeling of identity in knowing who your mother is – I can live without knowing who my father is.

Looking back, I realise I always felt outside the family. I was treated differently from my younger brothers and I could never figure out why I had no identity as a daughter.

I felt guilty all the time – and now I think it was for being born. Because my stepmother seemed to blame me for everything, I felt responsible for her unhappiness. No effort on my part made any difference. Once I tried to have an honest talk with her but she wouldn't listen.

My stepfather lived a violent and isolated life. I was sexually abused by our landlord with my stepmother's tacit co-operation. She told me he would throw us out of our lodgings if I said anything. Later my stepfather abused me too. I hated him to the point where I could not even shake his hand or say his name in prayer.

When I was 35 and had a family of my own my stepfather was in hospital with his third heart attack. He asked to see me alone. I can still remember how afraid I was. He was sitting on the side of his bed, tears streaming down his face. I didn't want to care. He looked at me and said, 'I'm sorry.'

I had the clear persistent thought, 'Touch him.' I put my hand on his shoulder and said, 'It's all in the past – it's all right.' And I meant it.

Then he said, 'Whatever time I have left I am going to devote to making things up to my wife.' For the remaining six months of his life he did that – and much more. He and my stepmother died within ten days of each other.

I have one picture of my real mother. She was wealthy, spoiled and beautiful and died after living what the world saw as a wasted life.

What has hurt most is not the fact of being illegitimate, but the fact that we never faced it as a family. Discovering the truth has explained my past and made me really free for the first time.

Chapter 7

From despair to hope

'Marriage breakdown is the number one psycho-social problem of our time,' says Jack Dominian, director of the Marriage Research Centre in London, England.

'When marriage breaks down the sheer cost in terms of human misery is enormous,' comments Maureen Green in her book *Marriage* (Fontana, 1984). 'The tears, the depressions, the suicide attempts pile up into a mountain of national agony.'

In this chapter three couples tell how they saved their marriages from the brink of disaster.

First love

Frances and Tony are both artistic and musical. She is a primary school teacher; he teaches mentally and physically handicapped adults. They live in a big old house in Canada with their three children, and Frances's mother and sister and her family. Frances writes:

I lay in bed, tossing and turning in the darkness, searching for an answer to the friction which was destroying our marriage. There always seemed to be terrible tension between us, simmering under the surface, ready to erupt at any moment, like Mount St Helens.

I felt such a failure. Humanly, I had everything I could possibly want in life – a husband, three lovely children, a nice house and a job which I loved. We had had such high hopes when we got married, but now I was desperate enough to consider leaving Tony. When had it all started to turn sour? What on earth would ever make things come right?

I was too disturbed to sleep. I prayed

Peter Mulder

87

desperately, 'O Lord, mend our love.'

After that prayer, I felt God started to work to remake our marriage – but it became evident that a lot depended on whether or not I was prepared to listen to Him and obey Him. With the openness of someone who had no alternative, I asked, 'O God, what would you have me do with my life?' I got an answer, crisp and clear, 'You need to learn to cope with your husband.'

I brushed the thought aside. Of course husbands and wives had to cope with each other, that was obvious. But how? In the end I said, 'I will try, but You have to show me how.'

A sort of revelation followed. I suddenly realised that from the time we started to have children ten years before, I had cut off my original relationship with Tony. It was as if I couldn't be a mother and a wife at the same time. Now the children came first, the family second, and Tony last, even after the dog sometimes.

The next day was a Sunday and as usual there was a mad rush to get to church on time. I had to stay home because one of the children was ill. Tony and the other two children set out on foot past our kitchen window, where I was washing up. I looked up just in time to see them sauntering down the road, the two children on either side of Daddy, arms linked and obviously talking about something with great enjoyment.

A feeling of intense rage and frustration rose within me. Sauntering! As if they had all the time in the world – why weren't they running or at least hurrying?

It suddenly hit me – 'But that is the man you fell in love with'. It was true. One of the first things that had attracted me to him was his easy-going enjoyment of life, taking things as they came whatever the circumstances. It was the way God had made him and I used to love him for it. Now I was condemning him for it.

I felt so ashamed and sad and sorry. Similar things came to mind, that I had pushed aside in order not to upset the family peace. How often I had squashed his sense of fun and adventure by telling him to be 'realistic', which really meant that I wanted to be in control of the situation. Oh dear, there were so many things to put right! I felt very humble and at the same time relieved and somehow free.

Fortunately, Tony is a forgiving person. When I found the courage to tell him these things, he reached out to me in forgiveness and I could sense a flicker of hope in him. He had been so hurt by my attitude over the years, that he needed to see that I meant business before he could trust in my love again.

A few weeks ago we were washing up together, both tired after a long day. During our conversation the old tension of the past arose. I could see the same old situation – barriers between us, mounting irritation and silent misunderstanding. Suddenly I put down the tea-towel and went up to him, put my arms around him and said, 'I don't want to be like this any more. I'm sorry.' Tony looked at me as if he could not believe what he was hearing. He knew I was serious.

For so long I've tried to control the destinies of my family, especially the children. Sometimes I call it 'wanting the best' for them and so feel justified in striving ruthlessly towards the achievement of this or that goal in their lives.

I have been working on this and I find there is a gradual loosening of my grip on their lives. It's a lifelong battle, to keep on the course God has laid down for us. I gladly undertake it – to free the children from the oppression of a dominating mother and Tony from the hurt of a demanding wife.

Happy ever after?

Reg and Jean live in a small British village where Jean manages the post office. They have two teenage sons. Jean went to ask her vicar for help with their marriage. She was shattered by his response:

'You've been coming here now for about seven weeks,' he told me. 'All I've been hearing is continual carping about how awful it has been for you being married to Reg, how mean and bad-tempered he is. I'm fed up with hearing the same old thing week in and week out. I don't want to hear any more. Before we go on, I want you to go into the church and ask God to show you just what life must have been like for Reg and why he's become as he is . . .'

I was dumbfounded. How could a man who called himself a priest be so unchristian and insensitive? He obviously didn't care. He probably hadn't believed a word I'd been saying about Reg. And of course he was a man – men do stick together. He probably thought it was the woman's fault, as always!

I went into the church. It was hot and stuffy outside, so the coolness was welcome, but I couldn't settle down because of the resentment boiling up from inside. Why should I sit and wonder what the marriage had been like from his side? He was fine. Weren't his meals given to him, his washing and ironing done for him? Didn't he have what he wanted – an unpaid housekeeper and a bed companion?

My thoughts eventually turned to the first months of our marriage and before, when, no doubt about it, we were happy. I suppose most pre-marriage relationships seem blissfully romantic. Ours did seem to be a happy alliance, we had so much in common – we liked riding, walking in the country, visiting places of interest, we shared a sense of humour and fun. But it all went wrong – why?

For a start, the relationship was marred by a pregnancy which neither of us wanted and which our parents knew nothing about. Our son was secretly looked after by a foster parent until we got married, when he was nearly one.

When we got married, Reg was a partner, with three others, in an advertising company which designed illustrations for packaging. He was the one who found the orders. The other partners were rather apt to misspend the money. Added to this was the fact that many large clients didn't settle their accounts for three to six months. This proved to be disastrous for a small company fighting for its survival. Two months after we got married, the firm went bankrupt and Reg found himself out of a job.

I had also lost my job. I had been working with horses in Hertfordshire and in return my employer had let us live rent-free in a flat. But during our honeymoon I had a show-jumping accident and landed up in hospital. I couldn't carry on my job – and so we were given notice to quit the flat.

On top of all this, Reg's mother collapsed and died suddenly, two days before a family gathering where we were going to introduce our son to our parents. Reg was deeply shocked. I was in a spin, with no idea how to cope with a grief-stricken husband and a youngster who was getting used to new surroundings.

Blair Cummock

'After we lost our jobs we emigrated to Cornwall in the hope of finding employment.'

After we both lost our jobs, we put our furniture in store and 'emigrated' to Cornwall in the hope of finding employment. But that didn't work out. We had to give the idea up and come back to live with Reg's father in his small, dark house in London. Reg had to go on the dole until he managed to find a job.

As I sat there in that church, looking back into the past, it slowly dawned on me how all this must have affected Reg. His dreams had all been shattered in two short months – firm collapsed, mother dead, home gone – and he was back where he had started. He must have felt an utter failure. No wonder he seemed to turn against me and his son. He had to use us as a fuse or he would have blown his mind.

I'd never before thought about any situation from another person's viewpoint. I'd never experienced such hurt as I now began to feel on Reg's behalf – my own hurts, hates and frustrations seemed nothing in comparison. Tears ran down my cheeks for him and all the unspoken feelings which he'd obviously had no idea how to cope with.

When I talked to the vicar he told me that he had had to force me to face the past because he believed I had to lose my fear of Reg before any change could take place. I had been afraid of his moods and I felt that my love for him had gone, driven out by his constant nagging and complaining, his moodiness and his awful temper which could explode at a moment's notice for no apparent reason. How could I find the strength to give him a solid relationship, which he could depend on?

'If you find it so difficult to love him, start with the things in him you still love, or loved in the beginning,' said the vicar. 'Build on that.'

It wasn't easy. There were times when Reg tried my patience, love and even my sanity. I had to discover whether there was anything to rescue and if it was worth carrying on. I remembered something I had learnt years before – the difference between merely doing the washing and ironing as a chore and doing it out of love; because no matter what I feel, God loves the other person for what he can become.

One day Reg was furious because I was going away for a weekend's retreat. He thought I was becoming a religious freak, shirking my responsibilities in the home. He threatened to see the vicar and tell him exactly what he thought of him. I thought it would be a good idea if he did. So he went to the vicar, and I went on the retreat.

Three months later the vicar suggested to Reg that he should seriously consider getting confirmed. He agreed. Our marriage began to mend, hurts began to heal and a sound relationship began to form between us.

Our elder son knows he is a year older than our marriage. It's important that he knows we really are his parents – and that we didn't have to marry because of him. Otherwise he might think all our problems are his fault. At the same time I don't want him to think what we did was right – or justifies him doing the same.

A good relationship doesn't mean that one partner gives in to the other because the other is stronger. I refuse to be the weak female needing the strong male to lean on. And I think it's important that we continue with our own interests – I am fascinated by historical research and Reg is a keen photographer.

You have to learn to accept – not to push your partner beyond his or her limits – and to bring out the best in each other. And because marriages, like cars, need continual maintenance, you can never say 'and so they lived happily ever after'. People change and grow, and needs develop.

Vendetta! **Mario and Linda's marriage was**

tempestuous from the start. At one point they fought over their children in the street outside their flat. Now they help other couples who are in difficulties – and their flat always seems full of extra children, who are staying with them while their parents sort things out.

Mario is Italian, overflowing with life, humour and drama. He runs an up-market hairdressing salon in London. Linda is Irish, quieter, but just as warm-hearted. I'll let them tell their own story:

Mario   We lived together for two years before we married. We were both making good money and as I had had a broken marriage before, I was happy to continue as we were. But after a while Linda started hinting about marriage and security and children.

I cancelled our wedding arrangements twice. Third time lucky – we finally made it. We were married in Ireland and everything was fantastic. When we went up to our honeymoon room with its big fourposter bed, Linda said, 'My mother says that if we don't settle my weekly allowance now, we never will.'

'You can't be serious!' I said. But she was. Still, we didn't settle it then.

Linda thought we should have children right away – at 29, she said she was getting old. Soon Diana and Carlos were born.

Those were my formative years. I wanted to prove to myself that I wasn't just going to be a hairdresser. And I wanted to prove my father wrong. When I gave up my medical studies and went to Britain he had told me that I would soon come home begging. I used to tell people that I was going to climb to the top and anything that got in the way would be destroyed. I even felt that about Linda –

if she agreed with me, fine; if not, I would fight her. She used to say to me, 'You are always right and I am always wrong, so it's no use talking to you.' She wasn't going to put up with that.

Linda   In fact I was scared of him and his temper. He would come home in the evening and if he had had a bad day he would wipe his finger along the picture frames to see if there was any dust. If there was a toy on the floor, his aggressiveness would come out. We would all feel it. I would be very nervous and anxious to please him and make sure everything was all right.

Mario   I built up our financial security. But I had to work seven days a week because I got involved in so many things – an employment agency, flat-letting, a perfume company, tourism, clothes. I sold things from home on Sunday – and often wasn't home until three a.m. I didn't spend much time with the kids. As far as I was concerned Linda was there for the home and the kids; I never told her what I earned or did. People called me a workaholic. But even when I earned a lot I wasn't satisfied.

We spent our money on holidays and expensive goods. I thought it was quite normal to buy stolen goods – and Linda would get quite enthusiastic about the clothes I bought her on that basis.

But we were having a lot of rows. She had become a compulsive buyer. She would buy a pair of boots for £120, even though she had another two or three pairs at home. I discovered she was running overdrafts at the bank; she was using hire-purchase and even selling her clothes to buy new ones and then lying about it. I tried to please her, buying her happiness with money. But obviously something was missing.

By the summer of 1979, things had gone from bad to worse. We often fought and threatened to leave one another. Sometimes I would say, 'Well, if you want to go, then go.' But when it actually happened my reaction was, 'Vendetta! I'll show her!'

In Ireland on holiday she told me she was going to leave me. I tried to persuade her not to. She said, 'You've never told me you love me.'

Linda   He said, 'There's nothing wrong which cannot be rectified.'

'There is,' I said. 'There's an awful lot wrong.'

We came home and talked a lot, but to no avail, and so I packed our things and left for Ireland with the children. He went through everything to make sure I didn't take anything which belonged to him.

Mario   The children were confused; they were then five and three. I began to feel uncomfortable. I was to fly over to Ireland to see them every two or three weeks. I said to Linda, 'We'll get a divorce, but before we settle anything, I want you to know that I feel really lost.'

'Why don't you try to find God?' she said.

I thought, 'What on earth is she talking about?'

I was soon lost in a deep depression. I didn't bother about the house or the business, I started to think about suicide. I began to feel guilty about my past, starting from when I was a child. When I told a friend, Andrew, about this, he said, 'Why don't you put all your problems in God's hands?'

'He doesn't want to know about me after all I've done,' I said.

'God isn't someone up there who judges us by a points system – "You down there, minus three, you minus seven",' he said. 'He is there to love us and help us if only we are willing to let Him.'

'Do you love your wife?' Andrew asked me, another time. I said I did. 'Then perhaps you should ask God to look after her and make sure yourself that you don't feel vengeful and help her in any decision she wants to take,' he said.

'What do you mean?' I demanded. 'If she wants a divorce, am I supposed to make it easier for her?'

But somehow his approach made sense. I went on going to Ireland every two or three weeks and I talked to Linda nicely, giving in to most of her requests. I kept asking her to come back and I asked her to forgive me. Meanwhile things were becoming difficult financially. Less money was coming in and the move and my trips to Ireland were expensive.

I had a breakdown and had to go to hospital. After a few weeks I was discharged, but I had to go back into hospital two or three times and I was in a permanent state of depression. Then I started going to a mutual support group, an offshoot of Alcoholics Anonymous for people suffering from depression. I began to accept that even if I was away from Linda I could give her my friendship and do my best for the children.

Linda   At first it was all very nice on my own in Ireland. I was free of Mario and living a frivolous life. But after a time I became lonely. Many nights I just sat in front of the television after the children had gone to bed and cried my eyes out. My eldest sister used

Lars Rengfelt

'The children had suffered a lot from our separation.'

to come over sometimes and she started to talk to me about God and prayer.

After four months I decided to return to England because every time I thought about God I had this terrible conscience. I felt that if I didn't go back to Mario, I would always wonder if our marriage could have worked again. When Mario came to visit us I could see that he was less aggressive and more gentle. I didn't know whether the change was for real or whether he just wanted something.

The children had suffered a lot from our separation. Carlos had developed bad temper tantrums – he would lie on the floor and bang his head. Diana used to cry for Mario at night, and had started to wet her bed.

When Linda and the children came back I tried to do things to please her, like buying her flowers and presents and telling her I loved her, and I tried to spend time with the children. I read the whole Bible through and other spiritual books. But I was still depressed and Linda wanted to go back to Ireland again.

I made the children wards of court so that she couldn't take them out of the country. But two days afterwards, Linda tried to take them to the airport. I rushed downstairs into the street to stop her. A friend heard us screaming at each other and asked us into her house, where she calmed us down with cups of tea.

I had started going to Mass and confession, which I had not done for many years. I had asked God to forgive me, and I had begun to pray and ask Him for guidance. One night over dinner a friend asked me if I had made restitution for some of the things I had done. 'I might have to go to prison,' I said. 'Do I have to do it?'

'Yes,' he said.

I thought he was mad. After that talk I took two tranquillisers.

In the end I went to confession and I told the priest, 'Look, I have all this silver which I bought and some of it I think was stolen and some wasn't. I don't know which is which. What shall I do? I want to give it back, but I don't know whom it was stolen from.'

'Bring me everything you think was stolen and I will give it to the police,' said the priest. I told Linda. She was stunned.

I filled up two huge plastic bags with silver, Wedgwood and other things. I told Linda I wanted to return a mink coat I had given to her, but she said, 'That's up to me.' I gave the bags to the priest and I didn't have to go to prison.

I had to change my business dealings. I told my manager I wanted to put my book-keeping right and declare everything honestly. I had been keeping three sets of accounts before that. And I stopped accepting deals which I knew weren't kosher.

During this time I was living in a flat upstairs, while Linda and the children were in our flat two floors below. I had come to accept the situation and was gaining in self-sufficiency and confidence. I wasn't going to force my way with Linda.

Linda had started to wash my shirts and tidy my room. Then one day she came upstairs and asked me to come down to her. She wanted my company. At the end of the evening she said, 'Why don't you stay down here?' Shortly afterwards we all went on holiday to Italy.

Linda   It took Carlos about six months to get cured of his temper after we got back together again. When we came home from Italy, Diana's teacher told us she had never seen a child change so much in three weeks. She used to be scared at school and stand in a corner by herself during playtime. Now both children have become confident, because they know they are loved.

Before, when Mario and I were fighting, Diana would keep on playing quietly, pretending she didn't notice, or she'd leave the room. Now if we disagree she smiles broadly and says, 'You aren't starting a fight, are you?' We all start to laugh. They never take sides. Mario is popular with their friends because he plays with them when they come to our house, or takes them swimming.

Mario   In October Linda became pregnant again.

101

Some time afterwards, I had another breakdown. Later it was discovered that there was a chemical imbalance which was triggered off when I got upset about anything. This time I was worried about how to support the new baby.

Linda's attitude was so different from the past, when she had hated my psychiatrist and told me to pull myself together. Now she showed a lot of strength and concern, and even came with me when I went to see the psychiatrist.

The last two or three years have been the best of my life. The baby is a rascal but a great joy.

Linda   Some time ago I went to Ireland for a family wedding and took the famous mink coat with me. When I came home Mario told me he was going to give me a new fur coat for Christmas. 'Isn't that funny!' I said. 'I've just given the other one to someone back home who I felt needed it more than I did.'

Mario   Whenever we are with a couple who are about to split up, we tell them what has happened to us. We find real satisfaction in trying to help others together. Having time for people comes before my work now.

Linda   Last summer, when we were on holiday in Italy, we were getting on each other's nerves. The noise of the children and neighbours was driving me crazy. Up till then I had not wanted to tell Mario when things were bothering me for fear that he would have another breakdown. But this time I felt I would explode if I didn't tell him.

One day in the car I blurted out all the things I had been bottling up. The result was amazing. Mario told me all he had been feeling and we found we could discuss everything as two rational human beings without getting upset or losing our tempers.

New horizons

A new world is home-made.

There are no schools – so far – where people can learn how to have a happy marriage. The only school is the example of our parents. I was lucky enough to grow up in a happy home. My parents have now been married for 56 years and while they have had their share of difficulties, they firmly believe marriage is forever. They are united by their love of God and their concern for the needs of the people around them.

How we live at home is not just a personal matter. A well-known American columnist told a friend of ours some years ago, 'The worst thing that has happened to America is not Vietnam or Watergate, but the breakdown of our family life.'

A fifteen-year-old hooligan told his teacher, 'My mother went to live with the man next door. When that happens to you, you want to smash everything.' How much of the violence on American streets and British football terraces can be traced to the falling apart of a secure home life? Meanwhile the drug industry worldwide makes millions out of the hopeless and confused products of unhappy homes.

'The future of your society, the future of humanity, passes by the way of the family,' Pope John Paul II told couples renewing their marriage vows in York in 1982. 'Make sure that your families are real communities of love. Allow that love to reach out to other people, near and far. In this way you will build up your society in peace, for peace requires trust, and trust is the child of love, and love comes to birth in the cradle of the family.'

Many of the people who tell their stories in this book are now applying the qualities they have learned through their marriages in their jobs and in helping other people.

Others have found themselves involved in their communities in new ways. A couple I know in the North of England were deeply concerned about Britain's racial and class divisions. They began to work with friends of all races to bridge the gaps between the communities in their city. Then the wife, who suffered deeply as a child during the Depression, wrote a play, partly based on her own experience of finding an answer to bitterness. It has been performed in schools and community centres all over Britain – helping people to face up to their prejudices and to understand what other groups feel.

Some other friends, in the province of Quebec, Canada, worked to bring together the opposing sides in a strike which had been going on for months in their town, tearing the community apart and creating unemployment. There were three couples involved – one runs a carpet factory, another pair are teachers, and the third husband is a former boxing champion who has recently begun to find a faith in God. Since the strike ended, they have gone on working together – trying to create a climate of co-operation, rather than confrontation, in their town and to spread this new spirit throughout the country.

Some years ago, when we visited Brazil, Paul and I met Henrique, the president of a shanty town on the outskirts of Rio de Janeiro. Thousands of families lived there in tin shacks, often without water or sewage. Sometimes when it rained heavily the shacks would collapse and slip down the steep hillside on which they were built.

At that time Henrique was living with another man's wife, went around with two knives and a gun in his belt, and was cheating his people by overcharging them for electricity. Later he put his life in order, making peace with the man who had wanted to kill him, returning to his wife and stopping swindling the community. He and his former enemies then went to the government with a plan for rehousing 250,000 families. The plan was accepted and implemented, and today the families are living in new clean apartment blocks with running water.

I believe that God has a plan for each of us – as individuals and as couples – and that if we try to find it, we may be surprised where it leads. For Paul and me it is simply a question of opening our eyes and hearts to the needs around us.

We can't blame everything on the government, management or the unions, on America or Russia. It takes all of us to put right what is wrong in the world, starting at home to build a society which works.